This book is dedicated to our two dogs, Claude and Dusty.
They've never met but woofed together through many hours
of video calls, and will enjoy chewing the pages.

M.O. & T.A.

First published 2022 by Walker Books Ltd
87 Vauxhall Walk, London SE11 5HJ

2 4 6 8 10 9 7 5 3 1

Text © 2022 Matt Oldfield and Tanya Aldred
Cover illustrations © 2022 Tom Jennings
Inside illustrations © 2022 Alessandro Valdrighi

The right of Matt Oldfield and Tanya Aldred to be identified
as authors and of Tom Jennings and Alessandro Valdrighi
to be identified respectively as cover illustrator and inside
illustrator of this work has been asserted in accordance
with the Copyright, Designs and Patents Act 1988.

This book has been typeset in ITC Leawood
Printed and bound by CPI Group (UK) Ltd, Croydon CR0 4YY

British Library Cataloguing in Publication Data: a catalogue
record for this book is available from the British Library

ISBN 978-1-5295-0201-5

www.walker.co.uk

MIX
Paper from
responsible sources
FSC® C171272

ULTIMATE CRICKET SUPERSTARS

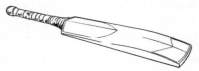

MATT OLDFIELD
& TANYA ALDRED

illustrated by Alessandro Valdrighi

WALKER
BOOKS

CONTENTS

ANYONE FOR CRICKET?

Hello! We're here to bowl you over with everything you need to know about 50 of the game's most entertaining superstars. 50 – that sounds like a lot, right? But actually, there are lots of different types of superstar in every cricket team. Some are better at either batting, bowling or catching, and some are brilliant at all three. In this book we've divided our superstars up into the six key cricket positions:

1 OPENERS Batters one and two – the brave ones who go first and face the fastest bowling

2 MIDDLE ORDER Batters three, four and five – the ones who get lots of runs and most of the glory

3 ALL-ROUNDERS The cricket heroes with the energy and excellence to bat, bowl and field

4 WICKET-KEEPERS They wear the gloves and they can catch pretty much anything

5 SPINNERS The slow-bowling magicians who can make the ball move in lots of different directions

6 FAST BOWLERS The super-speedy (and scary) bowlers with long arms, long legs and long run-ups

We also wanted to show you a wide range of superstars from all over the world, so 50 really isn't that many, is it? We could have picked 100, no problem! Each player is unique, but we've also broken them down into six categories:

1 LEGEND All-time greats

2 RISING STAR Young megastars

3 MODERN HERO Champions of today

4 ENTERTAINER Players with talent *and* personality

5 RECORD-BREAKER Stat superstars

6 GAMECHANGER Innovative pioneers

But before we introduce you to all our awesome superstars, we wanted to start with two very important messages about the sport they play. This goes out to everyone, but especially to readers who are new to the game. So, are you listening?

- Cricket is really fun and exciting!
- Cricket is actually pretty easy to understand.

You see, some people hear weird words such as "wicket" and "googly" and think, "Woah, cricket must be a really complicated sport." But it's not, we promise! And to prove it, let us present …

HOW TO PLAY CRICKET IN
SIX SUPER-SIMPLE STEPS

1 THE PITCH Two teams of eleven players meet on a pitch, usually outside and made of grass. One team bowls and fields, while the other team bats.

2 BOWLING Each bowler runs up and bowls (NOT throws – the arm has to stay straight) a small ball six times in a row. This is called an "over". The bowler's main aim is to get the batter out and take a wicket. One of the most satisfying ways of doing this is to hit the three wooden sticks (the stumps) that the batter is guarding. When that happens ... that's OUT!

3 FIELDING The other ten players who aren't bowling are fielders. One, the wicket-keeper, stands behind the stumps and the other nine are positioned all over the pitch. Their main jobs are to stop the ball, or catch the ball before it bounces.

4 BATTING Players bat in pairs, one at each end. The batter's main aim is to hit the ball – and score as many "runs" as possible. Here's how you score them:

- If the batter hits the ball in the air all the way over the boundary rope without it bouncing once ... that's 6 runs!

- If the batter hits the ball all the way to the boundary rope but it bounces or it touches the ground first … that's 4 runs!

- And if the batter hits the ball but not hard enough to reach the boundary rope, then the batters have to run between the two wickets. Each time they cross and reach the stumps at the other end … that's 1 run!

A batter stops batting when they're … OUT!
There are four main ways that can happen:

- **Bowled!** The ball hits their stumps.

- **Caught!** The batter hits a shot in the air and it's caught by a fielder.

- **Run out!** A fielder's throw hits the stumps before the batters have completed a run.

- **LBW (leg before wicket)!** The batter stands in front of their stumps, protecting them from being hit by the ball, but they can only do that with their bat and not with their legs. The bowler will often shout "Howzat?" in appeal to the umpire. If the ball would have hit the stumps but hits the leg instead … that's OUT!

5 TAKING TURNS Once ten out of the eleven batters are out (you have to bat in pairs, remember!), or they get to the end of their overs, that's the end of what's called an innings. The teams then switch roles.

6 WINNERS Whichever team finishes with the most runs wins the match. (Most of the time, anyway...)

Super-simple, right? We'll try our best not to use too many weird cricket words in this book, but any we do use will be explained in our handy Cricket Made Easy sections and in the glossary at the back.

SAY HELLO TO YOUR SUPERSTARS

So, are you ready to say hello to our 50 cricket heroes? Each of their stories is filled with interesting stats, funny facts, inspiring moments and, of course, exciting sporting drama.

OK, it's time to get this cricket party started. Please put your hands together and welcome our opening batters...

1
OPENERS

OPENERS

"So, who wants to go first?" It depends on the activity, doesn't it? If it's the queue at lunchtime or you're doing an exciting science experiment at school, the answer is obvious – "ME, ME, ME!"

However, when it comes to being a cricket batter, it's a little more complicated than that. On the one hand, it's a real honour to be chosen by your team to open the innings and it means you've got the maximum time available to score as many runs as you can. But on the other hand it usually means facing the fastest, scariest bowlers around, and right when they're at their most energetic and hungriest for wickets. And if you make one wrong decision or get beaten by a brilliant delivery? You're out, and your team is off to a terrible start.

THREE THINGS ALL
OPENERS MUST HAVE:

1 COURAGE Yes, you have to be very brave to stand there, the centre of attention, as someone big and tall charges towards you at top speed and then hurls a hard object in your direction.

2 QUICK REACTIONS As if facing really fast bowling isn't tough enough already, you've also got to concentrate on trying to hit the ball past the fielders. Openers have to watch each delivery really carefully, make a split-second decision about where the ball's going to land, and then think fast about what shot to play. To make things even more difficult, the ball is at its hardest and shiniest at the start of an innings, so it bounces, swings and moves more quickly off the pitch.

3 A VERY STRONG HELMET To deal with all the bouncers!

So, there you have it – the top secrets to becoming a successful opener. Sounds challenging, doesn't it? Put it this way; it really helps if, like Alastair Cook, England's leading opener, run scorer and century maker, you're someone who doesn't sweat!

THE SLOW OLD DAYS

In the old days, lots of things were way slower than they are now: cars, 100m sprinters and even opening batters. Before one-day internationals (ODIs) came along in 1971, the aim of most opening batters was pretty simple – it didn't matter what you did, or how slowly you scored runs, JUST DON'T GET OUT! As you can imagine, that led to a lot of dull defensive shots, a lot of **leaves** and some really, really long and boring innings. In 1977, for example, Pakistan opener Mudassar Nazar took 557 minutes to score a century in a Test match against England. Let us do a little maths to show you just how slow that is:

557 MINUTES That works out at over 9 hours, which is actually longer than the time it takes to fly in a plane from England to Pakistan! Can you imagine batting for all that time?!

100 RUNS IN 557 MINUTES So, on average, it took Nazar 5.57 minutes to score each and every run. There's a lot you can do in six minutes – for example, eat 22 bowls of rice and curry, like American world record holder Peter Czerwinski. Kids, please don't try that at home...

THE "LEAVE"

A "LEAVE" is where you let the ball go through to the wicket-keeper without even trying to hit it. Some batters do this by simply standing still with their bat raised high and out of the way, but others like to add a bit of style and extravagance.

Australian Steve Smith, for example, has been known to jump, twist and even swat the air like he's trying to trap a fly. And the best thing of all for a batter is that it really annoys the bowler!

WARNING: only leave if you know the ball is definitely NOT heading straight towards your stumps because that would be a super-embarrassing way to get out!

MORE RECORD (S)LOWS

557 minutes might sound like a long time to you, but not to these record-breakingly slow openers:

Longest-ever innings by a male opening batter:

970 MINUTES
Hanif Mohammad
Pakistan v. West Indies, 1958
(337 runs scored)

Longest-ever innings by a female opening batter:

594 MINUTES
Kiran Baluch
Pakistan v. West Indies, 2004
(242 runs scored)

Slowest-ever innings by an opening batter:

35 RUNS OFF 240 BALLS IN 332 MINUTES
Chris Tavaré
England v. India, 1982

THE FASTER AND MORE FURIOUS

These days, most openers don't spend days and days defending their stumps. In Test matches, modern players such as Australia's David Warner and India's Rohit Sharma take risks right from the start, while in T20 cricket, where each team only faces 120 balls, there's simply no time to waste.

It's all about scoring as many runs as you can, as quickly as possible, so you send your biggest hitters in first. In an Indian Premier League (IPL) match in 2013, West Indian whacker Chris Gayle scored a century off only 30 deliveries, and went on to score 175 runs in just 102 minutes. Now, that's a lot better than 9 hours, isn't it?

SO, WHICH KIND OF OPENER WOULD YOU BE?

Will you play or leave? Attack or defend? Go big and bold like Gayle or have people nodding off to sleep like Nazar? To help you decide here's everything you need to know about eight of the greatest openers cricket has ever seen, all with different styles and approaches. Then take our quiz to find out which of these superstars you would be.

JACK HOBBS
OPENER

COUNTRY: **ENGLAND**

CLUB: **SURREY**

DATE OF BIRTH: **16 DECEMBER 1882**

PLAYING STYLE: **RIGHT-HAND BAT**

NICKNAME: **THE MASTER**

SUPERSTAR MOMENT: **BECOMING THE FIRST BATTER TO SCORE 5,000 TEST RUNS**

FUN FACT: **EVERY 16 DECEMBER, A SPECIAL CLUB MEETS AT THE OVAL CRICKET GROUND TO CELEBRATE JACK BY ENJOYING HIS FAVOURITE MEAL: TOMATO SOUP, ROAST LAMB AND APPLE PIE.**

JACK HOBBS

Sir Jack Hobbs was born before cars were even invented! Can you believe that? Fortunately, cricket did already exist, and Jack quickly fell in love with the game, playing whenever he got the chance in the streets of Cambridge.

Jack grew up in a poor family, with eleven brothers and sisters, so when his dad became the groundskeeper at a local cricket club, Jack couldn't believe his luck. What an opportunity to make a career for himself! He spent his summers watching, learning and then practising his technique, using a tennis ball and a cricket stump for a bat.

As well as passion, Jack also had talent, and at the age of 21 he finally signed for a proper cricket club, Surrey, where he started working his way through the ranks until he became one of the best opening batters in the entire country. In 1908, Jack was called up to play for England and he scored an excellent 83 on his debut against Australia, featuring eight stylish fours and zero sixes.

Remember, this was long before the days of ODI cricket, let alone T20Is! The only international cricket was Test match cricket, and batters were judged by the number of runs they scored, and not the speed of their innings. That was perfect for Jack, who loved nothing more than batting for as long as possible. Once he got in, it was almost impossible to get him out. He was brilliant against both fast bowling or spin, and he could score runs in all weather conditions, even in the rain! The man they called "The Master" made batting look so effortless and easy.

Unfortunately just as Jack was reaching the peak of his powers the First World War broke out. By the time Test cricket returned six years later he was already 38 years old. Time to retire? No way! Jack came back batting better than ever, making:

- two heroic centuries against Australia in the Ashes in 1920–21
- three more against Australia in 1924–25
- 159 against the West Indies
- 211 against South Africa in 1924 at the astonishing age of 41.

What an achievement!

Jack batted on for another six years, becoming the first batter ever to reach 5,000 Test runs and the oldest player to score a Test century. He finally waved goodbye to international cricket in 1930, with fifteen centuries, an average of almost 57 runs per innings, and a special "Three Cheers" from his Australian opponents.

But Jack's cricketing days didn't end there. He played on for Surrey for another four years, finishing with an unbeatable total of 199 centuries and 61,760 runs. And he would have scored even more if he hadn't been such a nice guy – once he reached 100, Jack would often get himself out on purpose to give others a go!

Thanks to his winning combination of skill and kindness, Sir Jack became the first cricketer to be knighted by the Queen in 1953. He died in 1963 at the age of 81, but his legend lives on. In 2000, he was named as one of the top five cricketers of the twentieth century.

MITHALI RAJ

OPENER

COUNTRY: **INDIA**

CLUBS: **HYDERABAD, RAILWAYS, AIR INDIA WOMEN**

DATE OF BIRTH: **3 DECEMBER 1982**

PLAYING STYLE: **RIGHT-HAND BAT, LEG-BREAK**

NICKNAME: **CAPTAIN COOL**

SUPERSTAR MOMENT: **MITHALI IS THE WOMAN WITH THE MOST ODI RUNS EVER**

FUN FACT: **MITHALI LOVES READING!**

MITHALI RAJ

When Mithali was a little girl, what she loved best of all was a type of Indian classical dance called Bharatanatyam. Every day she danced, in the kitchen, on the way to school, until her toes and ankles hurt. She wasn't very interested in boring old cricket at all.

Then one summer she was sent to a cricket camp by her dad, who was fed up of Mithali daydreaming her way through the holidays. She showed some flair, joined the school cricket team, and her dad decided that Mithali would be a cricketer. Just like that!

This meant making a choice between dancing costumes and cricket bats, and when Mithali was called up as a standby for the World Cup in 1997, aged only fourteen, cricket won.

By the time she was sixteen, she'd played in her first one-day international against Ireland in Milton Keynes. She opened and made 114. Imagine doing that in year eleven! Three years later, in 2002, she was back in the UK during a tour in which India didn't win a match. Disaster, darling! The one golden moment was during the second

Test when nineteen-year-old Mithali made 214, then the highest Test score ever by a woman. She didn't realize that she had broken the record until one of her teammates was sent on the field to tell her! By the next World Cup she was captain and her 91-not-out in the semi-final guided India to the final – where they were thrashed by Australia.

But all this time, while she was leading her country and elegantly stroking the ball all over the place, she hadn't fallen in love with cricket. It wasn't until 2009, ten years after her debut, that she actually started enjoying the game rather than doing it to prove something to her dad.

Mithali is the best female batter to have come out of India, a very elegant player to watch, with dainty footwork and long languid strokes through gaps in the field, particularly through the covers. She is also famously calm both at the crease and in the dressing-room. During the World Cup final at Lord's in 2017 she was seen sitting serenely on a chair reading a book while waiting to bat! A Mithali Raj emoji was also top of the charts on social media during the same competition.

Mithali has been an inspiration, particularly for young Indian girls, and she became the first female cricketer whose international career spanned two decades, starting when female cricketers played for nothing in empty grounds to today when they can make good careers out of the game and play in front of packed stadiums. She recently gave up T20s in the hope of prolonging her career a little longer. We hope she plays for a lot longer. What a trailblazer!

TAMMY BEAUMONT

OPENER

COUNTRY: **ENGLAND**

CLUBS: **KENT, LIGHTNING, LONDON SPIRIT, SYDNEY THUNDER**

DATE OF BIRTH: **11 MARCH 1991**

PLAYING STYLE: **RIGHT-HAND BAT AND OCCASIONAL WICKET-KEEPER**

NICKNAME: **TAMBO**

SUPERSTAR MOMENT: **BEING NAMED PLAYER OF THE TOURNAMENT IN THE 2017 WOMEN'S WORLD CUP**

FUN FACT: **HER GYMNASTICS COACH NICKNAMED HER "THE MIGHTY ATOM" AS SHE WAS SO SMALL.**

TAMMY BEAUMONT

Tammy was just eight when she persuaded her dad
that she could fill the gap in his U-11's cricket team.

Skip forward eighteen years and that girl is
a star! She's a World-Cup winner with England and
had the honour of being named the 2017 player of
the tournament. Perhaps even more excitingly, she
has changed the way that English female batters
look at the game. How about that as a triple
achievement!

England women opening batters used to
be very careful and correct, but Tammy wasn't
interested in batting like a steam train, she was
an express. Off she went – *whack*, *smack* – giving
England batters the kick they needed to spring
forward into the 21st century with a swagger. The
fastest hundred ever by an Englishwoman? By
Tammy, of course: off 47 balls against South Africa
in 2018!

Things haven't always been straightforward,
though. There were stops and starts along the way,
and for the first seven years she batted at every
position except number 4. She nearly gave up the
whole thing to set up a sports massage business

after a miserable World Cup in 2014, but decided to have one more go. And this time she was going to be an opener. What a good decision!

She was trusted to replace her hero, the great Charlotte Edwards, in the opening slot, and made big runs against Pakistan. Then came the World Cup – the runs and the glory – then an amazing spell in 2018, when she made three international hundreds in ten days! At the end of that summer she had put together a record 628 runs for England at an average of 57 runs per innings – another year, another achievement.

England experimented with her batting in the middle order for the T20 World Cup in Australia, which didn't quite come off, and she looked forward to returning to her familiar opening role. As did England's fans. As everyone knows by now, you should never underestimate the pocket rocket!

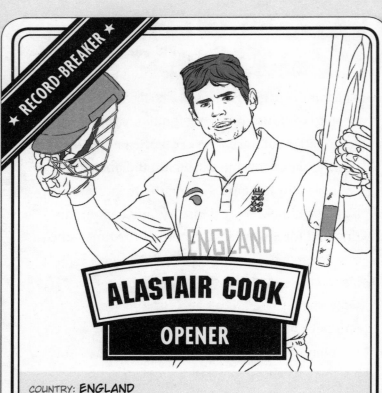

ALASTAIR COOK

OPENER

COUNTRY: **ENGLAND**

CLUB: **ESSEX**

DATE OF BIRTH: **25 DECEMBER 1984**

PLAYING STYLE: **LEFT-HAND OPENING BAT**

NICKNAME: **CHEF**

SUPERSTAR MOMENT: **SCORING 294 AGAINST INDIA IN 2011**

FUN FACT: **HE CAN PLAY THE PIANO, SAXOPHONE AND CLARINET.**

ALASTAIR COOK

Alastair Cook is your classic cool, calm opener. Despite playing really long innings in the scorching sun in some of the hottest countries in the world, scoring the highest number of runs and most Test centuries for England, having the most runs ever by a left-hander in Test history, and captaining England for 59 Tests – a record at the time – the guy doesn't sweat! His shirt always smells like it's freshly out of the washing machine – although we've never been quite close enough to sniff and find out for sure...

When Alastair was young, he loved two things: cricket and singing. When he was only eight, he became a chorister at London's famous St Paul's Cathedral, where he had to balance his school work and his singing – something that he said prepared him for the discipline of Test cricket. But as he grew older cricket hit singing for six, and by the time he was a teenager he was in the nets at 8 a.m. every day.

Alastair wasn't a batter with beautiful technique or a really exciting range of shots but, as we said earlier, that's not necessarily what being an opener is all about. What he could do really well was concentrate for hours and hours, protecting his wicket and keeping super-calm – an ability that carried him through many problems in his career.

He was a teenager when he made his debut for Essex and only 21 when he was called up to play for England, in India, where they were having an injury crisis. After three days' travel and battling jetlag, he made his debut and scored a hundred in the second innings. Pressure, what pressure?! Alastair learned to love the challenge of batting in India, Pakistan, Bangladesh and Sri Lanka, keeping things slow and steady as he went on to score more runs there than any other non-Asian batter.

And that was how he continued – a determined collector of runs, battling past the fastest bowlers in the world at the top of the innings. In 2010–11, he made 766 runs to help England win their first Ashes series in Australia for 24 years and, just under two years later, he'd scored the most Test centuries in English cricket history, and he was still only 27!

With such a cool head under pressure Alastair seemed the perfect choice to become the next England captain after Andrew Strauss retired, and he made centuries in each of his first five Tests in charge – what a start! He led England to some great victories, especially against India and Australia – but by 2016 he'd had enough of being captain and so he resigned. He continued opening the batting for England, though, under Joe Root, until September 2018, when he played the final innings of his final Test at The Oval. And how did he end his extraordinary England career? With yet another slow and steady century, of course! As he raised his bat the applause went on and on, spreading out into the summer's afternoon. What an outstanding opener!

The Queen knighted Sir Alastair a few months later and he continued to play for Essex, his boyhood club, and work on the family farm. And all without a whiff of a smelly armpit!

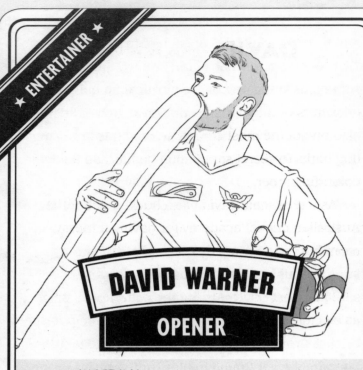

DAVID WARNER
OPENER

COUNTRY: **AUSTRALIA**

CLUBS: **NEW SOUTH WALES, SUNRISERS HYDERABAD**

DATE OF BIRTH: **27 OCTOBER 1986**

PLAYING STYLE: **LEFT-HAND BAT**

NICKNAME: **HUM-BULL**

SUPERSTAR MOMENT: **HELPING AUSTRALIA WIN THEIR FIRST T20 WORLD CUP FINAL AND BEING NAMED PLAYER OF THE TOURNAMENT**

FUN FACT: **FUNNY FAMILY VIDEOS MADE DAVID A *TIKTOK* STAR DURING LOCKDOWN.**

DAVID WARNER

As well as being one of the most exciting cricketers of the modern era, David Warner is also one of the most controversial. From bizarre dog barks to secret sandpaper, he has had a very colourful career.

As a teenager, David was chucked out of the Australian cricket academy for having a messy room but, just a few years later, aged 22, he was strutting out to open the innings for Australia in a T20 against South Africa. The crowd went crazy as he clubbed the ball all over the huge Melbourne Cricket Ground, wearing his custard-yellow kit. Soon he signed a deal with Indian Premier League (IPL) team the Delhi Daredevils – David was on the way!

Yes, he could smash the ball for six after six in one-day games, but could he also open the batting in Test cricket? Some said he was simply a slogger, but when Australia gave him a chance and his own baggy green cap, he soon proved them wrong.

A month after making his debut, he slam-dunked the fourth fastest Test century of all time, reaching it with a mammoth six, and celebrating by sprinting across the pitch and leaping into the air. What an incredible innings! Here was a Test opener like no other!

And the runs kept on coming in all forms of cricket. In 2015, he helped Australia to win the World Cup and he was named the new vice-captain of the Test side too. David's determination to succeed was really paying off, but unfortunately, sometimes he took things too far. In one match, David even tried to intimidate the South African batter Faf du Plessis by barking like a dog! And on the 2018 tour of South Africa, things went very wrong.

During the Cape Town Test David told young batter Cameron Bancroft to take a bit of sandpaper out on the field with him. "Sandpaper? How is that going to help?" you might be wondering. Well, by rubbing it on the ball you can rough up the surface and give your bowlers an advantage. But don't try this at home – ball-tampering is strictly forbidden by the laws of the game. And when the television cameras caught Bancroft shoving the sandpaper down his trousers, uh oh, they were in big trouble...

"Sandpapergate" shocked the cricketing world. The Australians were called cheats and it was a disastrous time for David. He was sacked as vice-captain, sent home, banned from playing for a whole year and from being Australian captain for life.

In that year off, David had a lot of time to reflect on his mistakes, and apologized to fans. When he returned for the 2019 World Cup he was very nervous for his first proper game back, against Afghanistan, and was booed all the way through the match. Two supporters even dressed up as sandpaper and sat on the balcony of a flat overlooking the ground! Despite all that, though, David showed his strength and skill to finish on 89-not-out.

That summer, back home, he also made a mammoth 335-not-out in a Test match against Pakistan – beating the record held by the most famous Australian of them all: Don Bradman! And in 2021 he scored a quick-fire 50 in the World T20 final against New Zealand, as Australia lifted their first Men's T20 World Cup. From villain to hero, what a brilliant bounceback!

CHRIS GAYLE

OPENER

COUNTRY: **WEST INDIES**

CLUBS: **JAMAICA, ROYAL CHALLENGERS BANGALORE, PUNJAB KINGS**

DATE OF BIRTH: **21 SEPTEMBER 1979**

PLAYING STYLE: **LEFT-HAND BAT, RIGHT-ARM OFF-SPIN**

NICKNAMES: **UNIVERSE BOSS, GAYLE FORCE, SIX MACHINE**

SUPERSTAR MOMENT: **BREAKING THE RECORD FOR THE FASTEST-EVER CENTURY IN AN IPL MATCH IN 2013, REACHING 100 RUNS OFF ONLY 30 BALLS!**

FUN FACT: **IN THE IPL, CHRIS HAS WORN THE NUMBERS 175 AND 333 IN HONOUR OF HIS HIGHEST SCORES IN T20 AND TEST CRICKET.**

CHRIS GAYLE

The West Indies have produced many brilliant
opening batters over the years – Frank Worrell,
Desmond Haynes, the great Gordon Greenidge. But
for pure entertainment and power we've decided
to go for the "Universe Boss" himself, Chris Gayle.
Although his style is not necessarily everyone's cup
of tea, when it comes to opening the batting with
a bang there's no one better.

Chris made his international debut way back
in 1999 but it took him a few years to find his best
form for the West Indies. At first, he kept getting
bowled or caught while trying to hit the ball as
hard as he could every time. So, did Chris change
his ways and become a more defensive batter,
taking quick singles instead? No way – he just got
better at making sure his big shots went all the
way over the boundary for six!

By 2002, Chris had become one of the most
explosive and exciting ODI openers in the world,
and when T20I cricket came along a few years
later, it felt like a game invented especially for
him. Twenty overs to score as many runs as
possible? Yes please, challenge accepted! In only

his fourth match Chris blasted his way to 117 runs off just 57 balls, the highest score in T20 history at the time. He also played a key part in helping the West Indies to win the ICC World Twenty20 trophy in 2012 and 2016.

So, what makes Chris such a successful modern opener? He's not known for his beautiful technique or fancy footwork; no, his batting is all about brute force, or "Gayle Force" as he likes to say. Time and time again his bold, attacking style has helped his team get off to a high-scoring start. And when he gets going, the West Indies almost always win. With his height, strength and excellent coordination, when he connects bat with ball it goes a long, long way, sometimes even out of the stadium and into nearby gardens! They don't call him the "Six Machine" for nothing (well, he calls himself that, actually...).

Chris is so calm that nothing fazes him, not even facing the fastest, scariest bowlers around. He's an over-confident character off the cricket field too, which can get him into trouble. He's THAT boy in your class. In 2016, he had to apologize for behaving inappropriately towards a TV reporter during a live interview in Australia.

During another interview Chris once famously claimed, "They say Chris Gayle is the best T20 player ever. That's what they say, right? There is no debate in T20 cricket about who is the best player … that's why I'm the Universe Boss, I'm the greatest!" As arrogant as that sounds, it's hard to argue with the stats. He holds the record for the fastest-ever century – off only 30 balls! – and in 2020, he became the first batter ever to score 8,000 runs and hit 1,000 sixes in T20 cricket.

As well as being the King of T20 cricket, Chris has shown that he also has the talent and concentration to star in longer games too. Basically, he just loves batting, and he's still the only player ever to score a Test-match triple-century (he has done it twice), an ODI double-century and a T20I century. Oh, and he has also taken over 250 international wickets with his clever off-spin bowling. So, whether you like him or not, Chris Gayle is a cricket superstar – and he knows it!

SHAFALI VERMA

OPENER

COUNTRY: **INDIA**

CLUBS: **SYDNEY SIXERS, BIRMINGHAM PHOENIX, HARYANA**

DATE OF BIRTH: **28 JANUARY 2004**

PLAYING STYLE: **RIGHT-HAND BAT**

NICKNAME: **SHAFALI**

SUPERSTAR MOMENT: **PLAYING IN THE T20 WORLD CUP FINAL IN FRONT OF 86,000 PEOPLE IN MELBOURNE**

FUN FACT: **SHE MADE HER INTERNATIONAL DEBUT AGED 15, THE YOUNGEST T20 INDIAN PLAYER EVER!**

SHAFALI VERMA

If you're searching for a teenage sensation, stop!
She's here, under your nose!

Shafali's story is like something out of a film.
She grew up in a conservative area of India but
was always determined to be her own person.
When she was six she demanded to have her hair
cut short and stood out from all the other girls with
their long plaits.

Her dad trained her alongside her
brothers, and when her older
brother Sahil was ill for an
U-12s tournament, ten-year-
old Shafali convinced him that
she could play instead! Girls
weren't allowed to play
cricket but her hair
was still short so no
one noticed. Guess
what happened!
She was brilliant
and won the
player of the
match award!

She carried on training, growing more nimble and stronger by the day. She and her brother would flip over tractor tyres for fun – imagine! – and her dad paid her five rupees for every six she hit. She scored buckets of runs for her state side Haryana and, aged only fifteen, was called up for India. She was out for zero in her first match, against South Africa.

Did that break her? Of course not! A month and a bit later, she made two 50s in successive matches against the West Indies, breaking her hero Sachin Tendulkar's record as the youngest Indian to make an international 50.

Her fearless approach to batting has made her a hero to lots of young Indians and she has scored more sixes in international T20s since her debut than anyone else. She loves to dominate during the power play and is an opening batter to reckon with. Virender Sehwag, the famous Indian batter who she has been compared to, has called her "a rockstar".

In the Women's T20 World Cup in Australia, which took place just before Covid closed down the world, she was on fire, scoring 163 runs at a cool strike rate of 158.2 (the average number of runs scored per 100 balls faced). The crowd loved her!

Now when her dad walks down the street, people stop him to say, *"Kya Sanjeev bhai, aapki beti ne to mahilao ka cricket dekhne pe majboor kar diya* [Your daughter has forced us to follow women's cricket]."

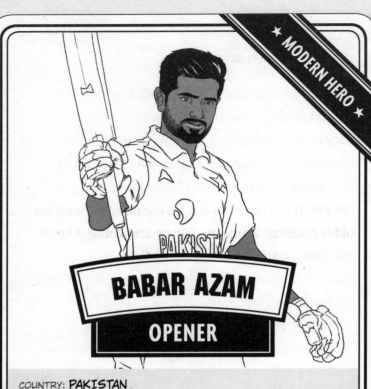

BABAR AZAM
OPENER

COUNTRY: **PAKISTAN**

CLUB: **KARACHI KINGS**

DATE OF BIRTH: **15 OCTOBER 1994**

PLAYING STYLE: **RIGHT-HAND BAT**

NICKNAME: **BOBBY**

SUPERSTAR MOMENT: **BECOMING THE TOP-RANKED BATTER IN THE WORLD IN BOTH ODI AND T20I CRICKET**

FUN FACT: **AGED THIRTEEN, BABAR WAS A BALL BOY AT THE GADDAFI STADIUM IN LAHORE, AND WHEN A SOUTH AFRICAN BATTER HIT A BIG SIX HE CAUGHT IT BRILLIANTLY!**

BABAR AZAM

So far, we've talked about openers who score runs slowly and others who score them very, very quickly. But if you're looking for someone in between, then Babar Azam is the batter for you.

He grew up in Lahore, Pakistan, playing cricket in the streets with his friends and with his older cousins: Kamran, Adnan and Umar Akmal. All three Akmal brothers went on to represent their country, but it was young Babar who would become the most successful member of the family.

By the age of eighteen Babar had already starred at two U-19 World Cups, opening the batting and top-scoring for Pakistan in both tournaments. It was clear that he was a superstar in the making, and three years later, in 2015, he finally got the call-up he was hoping for: to the senior one-day side! After scoring a stylish 50 on his debut against Zimbabwe, Babar never looked back. A year later he hit three hundreds in a row in an ODI series against the West Indies, followed by a 50 in his first Test match. With his calm head and classic cut shots and cover drives he is now Pakistan's number one batter in every form of cricket, as well as the national team captain.

Yes, Babar has that special ability to do it all: he's fearless when facing fast bowlers and excellent against spinners; he can bat patiently in Test matches and powerfully in T20Is. He's probably at his best, however, over 50 overs, where he can score steadily and build innings that are both elegant and exciting. In 2018, he became the second-fastest player ever to reach 2,000 ODI runs, in only 45 matches. Now, he's playing his way towards 5,000!

Babar doesn't always open the batting for Pakistan, but the shorter the cricket match, the higher he moves up the order. In Test matches he usually comes in at number 4, in ODIs at number 3, and in T20s he has become one of the greatest openers in the game. By going in first, Babar gets to face more of his team's 120 deliveries. That means he can take his time and play beautiful drives for four, rather than rushing to hit the big shots straight away. But don't worry, when Pakistan need quick runs, Babar can pull and sweep the ball for six too!

Whatever number he bats, Babar's greatest strengths stay the same: balance, timing, composure and consistency. In fact, as he gets older, his batting keeps getting better and better! People talk about cricket's famous "Fab Four" batters (Australia's Steve Smith, New Zealand's Kane Williamson, England's Joe Root and India's Virat Kohli), but many believe that it should be the Fab Five now because Babar is at that superstar level too.

In April 2021, he became the fastest player in the world to score 2,000 T20I runs, achieving it in four fewer innings than Kohli. A month later Babar overtook his Indian rival again to become the number-one-ranked batter in ODI cricket, and after scoring the most runs at the T20 World Cup in the UAE and Oman he also climbed to the top of the T20I chart. Can he complete the treble and become the number one Test batter too? We'll have to wait and see, but Babar certainly has lots more brilliant batting ahead of him.

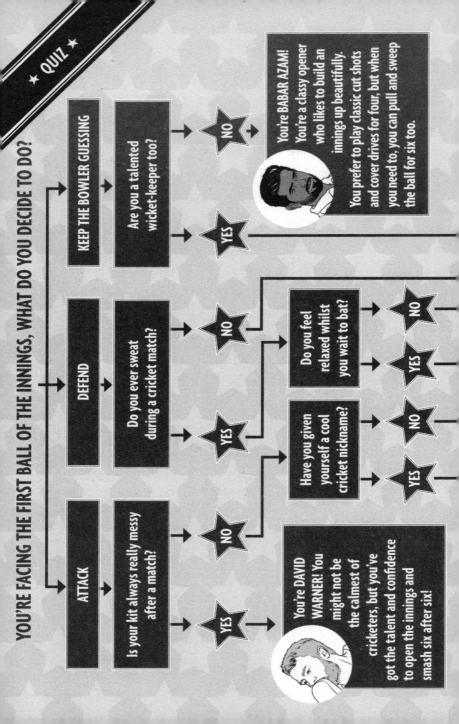

★ QUIZ ★

YOU'RE FACING THE FIRST BALL OF THE INNINGS, WHAT DO YOU DECIDE TO DO?

ATTACK

Is your kit always really messy after a match?

YES

You're DAVID WARNER! You might not be the calmest of cricketers, but you've got the talent and confidence to open the innings and smash six after six!

NO

Have you given yourself a cool cricket nickname?

YES

NO

DEFEND

Do you ever sweat during a cricket match?

YES

NO

Do you feel relaxed whilst you wait to bat?

YES

NO

KEEP THE BOWLER GUESSING

Are you a talented wicket-keeper too?

YES

NO

You're BABAR AZAM! You're a classy opener who likes to build an innings up beautifully. You prefer to play classic cut shots and cover drives for four, but when you need to, you can pull and sweep the ball for six too.

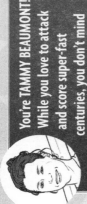

You're CHRIS GAYLE! For you, batting is all about power and entertainment, from your first ball to your last. You're a cricket superstar and you know it. Bowlers, beware!

You're SHAFALI VERMA! You've got your own fearless batting style, and you love to entertain, but the celebrity lifestyle isn't for you.

You're MITHALI RAJ! There's no need to stress about cricket; it's a game to be enjoyed! After a relaxing read, you like to go out and bat for as long as possible, while scoring lots of runs along the way.

You're TAMMY BEAUMONT! While you love to attack and score super-fast centuries, you don't mind taking your time and doing a bit of defending.

You're ALASTAIR COOK! A cool, calm opener, you could bat for days and days if they'd let you. Sure, you love scoring runs but the main thing is not getting out.

You're JACK HOBBS! You love cricket so much that you can't wait to open the batting for your team. Scoring sixes isn't really your style, but once you get in, it's almost impossible to get you out.

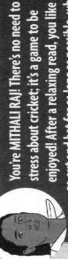

2
MIDDLE
ORDER

MIDDLE ORDER

After the two opening batters, come ... numbers 3, 4 and 5! Or as cricket folk like to call them ... the middle order. But don't think because they're in the middle that means they're average, or not as good as the openers. No, no, NO! In most teams the middle-order batters are just as good, if not even better.

Think of it this way: if your army was under attack, would you send out your most skilful fighters straight away? No, not if you were smart! Instead, you would start with a few of your biggest, bravest warriors and keep your star soldiers back, saving them for when you need them the most.

And it's the same with batting! Once the openers have battled past the fast bowlers at their hungriest for wickets, then the middle order come in and often steal all the glory.

THREE THINGS ALL MIDDLE-ORDER BATTERS MUST HAVE:

1 TOP TECHNIQUE To make it in the middle order you must be an absolute batting wizard. You have to be able to play every sensational shot in the cricket book, against every kind of bowling, and all around the wicket. And that's just the attacking part; when the batting gets tough, you need to be able to defend your wicket too.

2 FOCUS AND PATIENCE UNDER PRESSURE Every time you walk out onto the pitch you'll be expected to score lots of runs for your team and lead them to victory. That level of stress can sometimes lead to silly mistakes, so it takes a calm, confident character to create middle-order magic.

3 AN EXTRA SPRINKLING OF STAR QUALITY! Every middle-order batter has a different style – but one thing unites them all: class. They can dig in and tough it out when they have to, but they're also the big-time stroke-players that people really want to watch. Think of them as the lead singers of the band.

SENSATIONAL SHOTS

Earlier we said middle-order batters needed to master every shot in the cricket book. Here are the top five essential shots:

ON THE OFFSIDE
1 CUT If the ball is short and wide, step back and play the ball late, swinging the bat horizontally.

ON THE LEGSIDE
2 PULL If the ball is short and bouncing up above your waist, step back, rotate your body and swing your bat across, like you're swatting flies.

3 HOOK Same as the pull, but to be played against a ball that bounces even higher!

4 SWEEP Go down on one knee and sweep the ball around the corner behind you. Only play this shot against spinners unless you're feeling super-confident.

OFFSIDE, LEGSIDE AND DOWN THE MIDDLE
5 DRIVE Step forward to where the ball is about to bounce and swing the bat through, straight and powerful. Perhaps the classiest-looking shot in cricket.

"OFFSIDE" AND "LEGSIDE"

This is not to be confused with the offside rule, football fans! In cricket, the pitch where the batters stand is in the middle of the ground. The batters can hit the ball wherever they like, but to help explain where the ball has gone, and where the fielders should stand, cricket lovers divide the ground in half into two semi-circles.

So the batter can hit the ball into:

• "OFFSIDE": the big space your nose is pointing towards

• "LEGSIDE": the semi-circle of space behind your legs and bum. Some people call this the "on side".

Or, if you're a brilliant number 3, 4 or 5, you can play a beautiful drive straight down the middle!

CAPTAIN COOL

There's one other thing that a lot of middle-order batters have, and that's leadership skills. Yes, many of them don't just score most of the runs for their teams, they are often also the captains. Middle-order players are usually the best, and they're better at making judgement calls during a match.

Cricket captains have much more to do than football captains. They help choose the team and the batting order, decide on tactics and make decisions in the field – who to bowl, where to put the fielders, whether to defend or attack.

Most important of all they have to be lucky. Before a game the two captains toss a coin and choose whether to bat or bowl. It can be very important, depending on the weather or the pitch.

One of the most famous bad decisions was in 2002 when England were in the middle of an eighteen-year sequence of losing the Ashes. At the first Test at Brisbane, England captain Nasser Hussain won the toss and decided to bowl. At the end of the first day Australia were 364–2 – they won the match by a whopping 384 runs and the series 4–1. Whoops!

MIDDLE-ORDER RECORDS

To prove what we said earlier about star quality,
here are three of cricket's biggest batting records,
which are all owned by middle-order players:

Most Test match runs in a career:

15,921
Sachin Tendulkar
India [Usually No. 4]

Highest Test match score:

400
Brian Lara
West Indies v. England, 2004 [No. 3]

Highest Test match average:

99.94 RUNS PER INNINGS
Sir Donald "The Don" Bradman
Australia [Usually No. 3]

SO, WHICH KIND OF MIDDLE-ORDER BATTER WOULD YOU BE?

Would you be calm and classy, determined and
defensive, or exciting and explosive? Will you
stroke the ball for four or smash it for six? And
what will be your greatest, game-winning shot?
To help you decide, here's everything you need to
know about ten of the most amazing middle-order
batters cricket has ever seen. Then take the quiz to
find out which of these superstars you would be.

DON BRADMAN
MIDDLE ORDER

COUNTRY: **AUSTRALIA**

CLUBS: **NEW SOUTH WALES, SOUTH AUSTRALIA**

DATE OF BIRTH: **27 AUGUST 1908**

PLAYING STYLE: **RIGHT-HAND BAT, MIDDLE ORDER**

NICKNAME: **THE DON**

SUPERSTAR MOMENT: **SCORING 309 RUNS ON THE FIRST DAY OF THE THIRD TEST MATCH AGAINST ENGLAND IN 1930**

FUN FACT: **DON WAS ONLY DROPPED BY AUSTRALIA ONCE!**

DON BRADMAN

Imagine being the greatest batter who has ever lived. Well, that was Don Bradman. The only man to average nearly 100 runs each time he walked out to bat in a Test match. Just think about it – it's incredible!

In fact, Don was so good, so brilliant that he's still the only batter ever to score a triple Test century in a single day! He dominated the game so much that his opponents decided to create a whole new way of bowling, just to try to get him out. During the "Bodyline" series of 1932–33, the England captain, Douglas Jardine, told his bowlers, in particular Harold Larwood, to bowl leg-theory at Don. Leg-theory meant bowling very fast, very bouncy balls towards the batter's body at leg stump – meaning the batters had to:

a) play the ball and risk being caught by the ring of close fielders,

b) move away and risk being bowled,

c) duck and risk being hit.

Oh, and this was at a time when players just wore cloth caps on their heads, not big, padded helmets! A number of players were hit, the crowds filling the Australian grounds were furious, and Australia had no answer. England won the series 4–1 and Don's average fell to a less super-human 56.

But "Bodyline" had caused an international scandal. Bowling balls aimed at the batter's body – that just wasn't cricket! Leg-theory was banned, Jardine retired, and Larwood never played for England again. But Don? He played on and on – scoring run after run after run. His quick feet, calm manner and ability to switch from defence to attack and back again proved very difficult to deal with, and he was brilliant at hitting the ball into the gaps between the fielders – a huge advantage!

He was also made Australian captain, until the Second World War broke out in 1939. He served in the air force and army for a year, but he had to stop because of muscle pain. After that, he didn't expect to ever play for Australia again ... but he did. His last series was Australia's tour of England in 1948. By then he was 40 years old, but who cares about age when you're the best cricketer ever? His team became known as "Bradman's Invincibles" because during their four-and-a-half-month stay in England, they didn't lose a single match!

In his final Test innings Don only needed to score four runs to keep his batting average above 100. The packed crowd at The Oval and the England players applauded him to the middle, and the England players even gave him three cheers! But sadly, it wasn't to be. He was bowled for 0 to just his second ball. Oh well, an average of 99.94 runs would just have to do! Besides, imperfection is far more interesting than perfection (I'm not sure Don would have agreed with that)! As he arrived at London's St Pancras station to start his long journey home to Australia, hundreds of people lined the platforms to wave goodbye to cricket's greatest hero.

Not bad for a boy from the bush, who learned how to bat by endlessly hitting a golf ball with a cricket stump onto a water tank in the garden of his house. Sometimes keeping it simple works best!

How Don would have coped in the T20 era, we can only guess – he might not have been picked, as he hit only six sixes in his Test career! But there has never been anyone else like Don. Not only the most extraordinary batter of all time, but one of the most exceptional athletes ever.

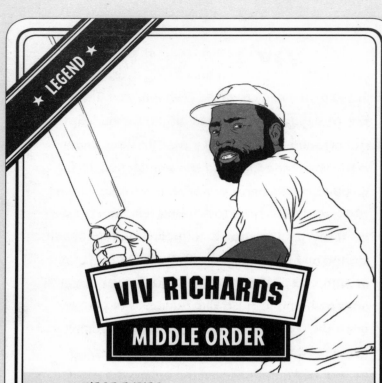

VIV RICHARDS

MIDDLE ORDER

COUNTRY: **WEST INDIES**

CLUBS: **LEEWARD ISLANDS, SOMERSET, GLAMORGAN**

DATE OF BIRTH: **7 MARCH 1952**

PLAYING STYLE: **RIGHT-HAND BAT**

NICKNAMES: **MASTER BLASTER, KING VIV**

SUPERSTAR MOMENT: **SCORING 100 OFF JUST 56 BALLS AGAINST ENGLAND IN 1986, A NEW RECORD FOR THE FASTEST-EVER TEST CENTURY THAT LASTED FOR 30 YEARS**

FUN FACT: **VIV ALSO PLAYED FOOTBALL FOR HIS COUNTRY, ANTIGUA AND BARBUDA, DURING THE QUALIFIERS FOR THE 1974 WORLD CUP.**

LEGEND ★

VIV RICHARDS

In 1973, 25 years after Don Bradman's famous last Test for Australia, a new young cricket star embarked on an exciting journey from his home in the West Indies to make a name for himself in England. Viv Richards would go on to become one of the most brilliant middle-order batters of all time.

When he first arrived in England, however, Viv started by playing local league cricket for a club in Bath. Not for long, though; he was so good that after one high-scoring season Somerset quickly gave him a two-year contract. On his one-day debut for the club he scored a match-winning 81-not-out, and his teammates even gave him a standing ovation as he left the pitch. A new cricket superstar had just arrived on the scene.

Viv made his international debut for the West Indies in 1974, and in only his second Test match he hit 192 not out against India, including twenty fours and six massive sixes! Woah, with that kind of big-hitting he was the perfect batter for the new one-day format, and a year later he was part of the West Indies team that won the first-ever Men's Cricket World Cup. That was, of course, an amazing moment for him, but really it was only the start for this superstar. Four years later Viv led his country to victory again in the 1979 Cricket World Cup, and this time he scored a stylish century in the final.

Poor England were blown away by Viv's brilliance, and that wasn't the only time. In an ODI in 1984, the West Indies were struggling at 166–9, but no matter what the English bowlers tried they just couldn't get their key man out. Viv went on to score 189 not out off 170 balls and win the game for his team, forming the highest tenth-wicket partnership in history with Michael Holding. Many people still call it the greatest ODI innings ever.

While Viv was a very powerful striker of the ball and he loved to score runs quickly, he was no simple slogger. Oh no, he could bat defensively when he needed to and he had the timing and technique to play shots all around the ground. And although he was at his best in ODIs (this was way before the days of T20, remember!), Viv's greatest individual achievement actually came in Test cricket in 1986. By then, he was the West Indies captain and during a 5–0 win over England (again!) Viv scored 100 runs off just 56 deliveries, breaking the previous record for the fastest-ever Test century with eleven balls to spare. It was such a remarkable innings that as Viv raised his bat a fan raced onto the pitch to hug him!

Yes, if there's one cricketer who made batting look both beautiful and easy, it was King Viv. By the 1980s most batters were wearing helmets, but not him. No, all Viv needed was his West Indies cap, and he let his tremendous talent do the rest. He wasn't afraid of anything, not even facing the fastest bowlers in the world. England's Devon Malcolm found that out the hard way in 1990 when Viv smashed his first two balls for six! Now that's what we call a cool cricket superstar.

Viv played the game with lots of style but he was much more than just an entertainer. He also had a real winning mentality and understood the importance of organization, team work and hard work. That's why he's the only West Indies captain to never lose a single Test series; and that's why in 2000 he was named alongside Don Bradman, Jack Hobbs, Shane Warne and Garfield Sobers as one of the Top 5 Cricketers of the Century.

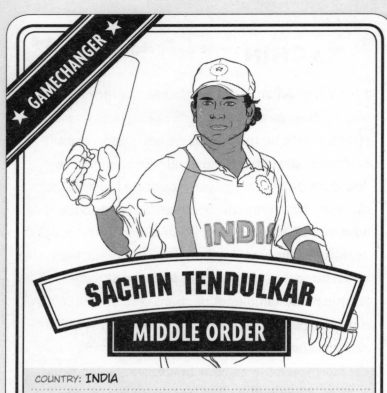

SACHIN TENDULKAR

MIDDLE ORDER

COUNTRY: **INDIA**

CLUBS: **MUMBAI, MUMBAI INDIANS, YORKSHIRE**

DATE OF BIRTH: **24 APRIL 1973**

PLAYING STYLE: **RIGHT-HAND BAT**

NICKNAME: **LITTLE MASTER**

SUPERSTAR MOMENT: **SCORING 98 RUNS AGAINST PAKISTAN IN THE 2003 WORLD CUP**

FUN FACT: **TENDULKAR WAS THE FIRST INDIAN CRICKETER TO HAVE A LIFESIZE WAX STATUE OF HIMSELF DISPLAYED AT MADAME TUSSAUDS IN LONDON.**

SACHIN TENDULKAR

Sachin Tendulkar may be only five foot five, but he was a colossus on the pitch. He was a baby-faced sixteen when he made his Test debut, but when he retired 26 years later he had scored 51 Test centuries in 200 Test matches and played 463 one-day internationals. A run machine for over a quarter of a century!

It is hard to imagine how famous Sachin was when he was at his peak. He would visit the temple in the middle of the night to avoid being mobbed by fans, and sometimes wore a fake beard and glasses so that he could watch a film in peace. His face was all over giant advertising posters and he turned cricket into a national obsession. The pressure must have been crazy! But Sachin soaked it all up – he is one of the greatest.

It all started when he walked out to make his debut against Pakistan. He only made a few runs but his teammates couldn't believe how brave this teenager was as he was peppered with short balls from the bowlers. The next year, aged seventeen, he made his first Test century, against England at Old Trafford, and when he was eighteen he played one of his very best innings, on a hurricane-fast pitch at the WACA in Australia, bashing 114 as the other Indian wickets clattered around him. He would go on to make at least 150 against every Test-playing nation, all round the cricketing universe, ending up with the most centuries and the most runs in both Test and ODI cricket. Not bad!

Sachin's success came from a combination of outrageous talent, endless practice, timing and a wonderful technique. He would play the ball very late and with perfect balance – *tonk* – a drive would have zipped to the boundary while your eyes were still concentrating on the batter. In fact, Don Bradman told his wife that Tendulkar reminded him of himself – the ultimate compliment!

As Sachin got older, he changed the way he played. He became less attacking and stopped playing some shots, but never tired of scoring runs. He captained India for a while and was a good teammate, helping the younger batters with their game. However, you have to feel sorry for whoever got out just before Sachin batted – any applause would be overshadowed by joyful shouts of

"Sa-chin, Sa-chin" and the sound of people banging the boundary boards in excitement.

Towards the end of his career Sachin's powers started to leave him, but there was time to win the World Cup with India in 2011 and hit his 100th 100 before he retired after his 200th Test in a huge celebration in his home city of Mumbai. Spectators cried and cheered as he said: "Time has flown by rather quickly. Memories like these are going to stay on with me forever. Especially 'Sachin, Sachin', that will reverberate in my ears until I stop breathing... Goodbye."

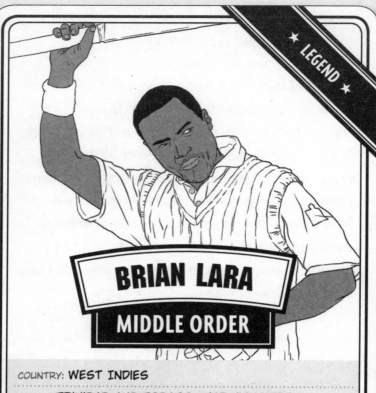

BRIAN LARA

MIDDLE ORDER

COUNTRY: **WEST INDIES**

CLUBS: **TRINIDAD AND TOBAGO, WARWICKSHIRE**

DATE OF BIRTH: **2 MAY 1969**

PLAYING STYLE: **LEFT-HAND BAT**

NICKNAME: **THE PRINCE**

SUPERSTAR MOMENT: **400 NOT OUT AGAINST ENGLAND OR 501 NOT OUT FOR WARWICKSHIRE AGAINST DURHAM. TAKE YOUR PICK!**

FUN FACT: **HE ONCE GAVE BARACK OBAMA BATTING TIPS.**

BRIAN LARA

Brian Lara ate runs for breakfast, lunch and dinner. He wolfed them down like home-made chocolate chip cookies still warm from the oven, more and more, quicker and quicker – he was never full! He wasn't content with 100 runs – he wanted 200, 300, 400. In fact, his highest first-class score is 501 not out – a world record that might never be broken!

Brian was a brilliant attacking middle-order batter. When he was in the right mood he was impossible to bowl at: his feet and hands moved so quickly and he could send the ball off at impossible angles to wherever the fielders weren't. Watching him at the crease when the bowler was running in was like watching a tiger hunting his prey, his knees bent, his bat high in the air waiting, waiting to pounce.

Brian was born in Trinidad, number ten in a family of eleven children. He used to practise by hitting a lime with a broomstick against the garage door over and over again, and no one who watched him as a child was surprised by what he became – one of the West Indies' greatest cricketers, and one of the best batters ever!

He had to wait until Viv Richards retired before he got a run in the side, but the West Indies fans didn't have to wait long to learn how good he was. In his fifth Test he scored 277 breathtaking runs against Australia at Sydney before being run out by a dodgy call by his batting partner! And he'd barely even got started.

In 1994, Brian beat Garry Sober's record Test match score, making 375 against England – his very favourite opponents. Two months later he beat the world first-class record when he thrashed his famous 501 runs in one innings for Warwickshire against Durham. He was dropped early on by the poor wicket-keeper who muttered to the slips, "Oh dear, he'll probably go on and get a hundred." Whoops! In that period he also became the first man to make seven hundreds in eight first-class innings.

Brian always had to be the best. In 2003, Matthew Hayden of Australia broke Brian's Test world record. Six months later Brian took it back at Antigua, this time making 400 not out! His opponents? England of course!

There were so many great innings, but probably the greatest of all was his 153-not-out in the fourth innings against the best-in-the-world Australians at Bridgetown in 1999, where he almost single-handedly got the West Indies over the line. As he pinged four through the covers to win the game, his teammates ran onto the pitch and the crowd went wild – it was one of the great fightbacks in sport.

Brian loved a bit of drama. By the time he retired from international cricket in 2007 he'd had a few tussles with the West Indies board, fallen out with some of his teammates, and been made captain before being sacked and reinstated – more than once! It was sometimes hard being a genius in a declining team, for both Brian and his teammates! But Brian had become such a cricket legend that he'd even had a computer game named after him – *Brian Lara Cricket*. Ask your parents.

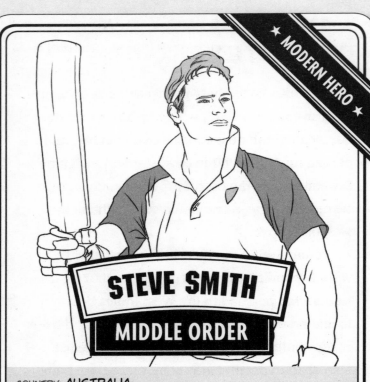

STEVE SMITH

MIDDLE ORDER

COUNTRY: **AUSTRALIA**

CLUBS: **NEW SOUTH WALES, DELHI CAPITALS, SYDNEY SIXERS**

DATE OF BIRTH: **2 JUNE 1989**

PLAYING STYLE: **RIGHT-HAND BAT**

NICKNAME: **SMUDGE**

SUPERSTAR MOMENT: **MAKING 774 IN THE ASHES SERIES AFTER SANDPAPERGATE**

FUN FACT: **HE HAS DUAL AUSTRALIAN AND BRITISH CITIZENSHIP, SO HE COULD HAVE PLAYED FOR ENGLAND. IMAGINE!**

STEVE SMITH

Steve Smith knows what it is like to be a hero. He also knows what it is like to be a zero. He has been called the best batter since Don Bradman, averaging around 60 in Test matches, but has also been booed as a cheat. What a strange career it has been for the man who just loves playing cricket.

Young Steve was obsessed with batting, he would spend two hours choosing a bat and, when he couldn't persuade anyone to practise with him, would head into the garage where his dad had hung a ball from the ceiling. Grown-up Steve is also obsessed with batting: playing shadow shots in the shower and netting for so long that he had to be asked to stop by worried members of the team management. Practising in the hotel room at night, keeping his teammates awake as the tap-tap-tapping of his bat travelled through the walls. Thank goodness players don't share a room any more!

Steve started his Test career as a leg-spinner who scored useful but awkward runs at number 8. After being dropped he worked on his game and, when he came back, his batting technique still looked a bit as if it had been put together by his grandad in the garden shed but – wow – it was effective. He scored hundreds for fun, settled in the middle order, and, helped by incredible powers of concentration, was nicknamed one of cricket's Fab Four batters alongside Virat Kohli, Joe Root and Kane Williamson.

He was made captain when Michael Clarke retired and continued on his merry way, scoring a hundred in India, described as the best ever by a visiting batter, before leading Australia to a 4–0 thrashing of England in the Ashes. Steve was the man of the series scoring 687 runs at an average of 137 – England didn't know how to stop him!

A few months later, on Australia's tour of South Africa in 2018, young batter Cameron Bancroft was caught on camera rubbing sandpaper on the ball to try and help it swing. Steve admitted he knew about the plan in advance and, alongside vice-captain David Warner, was sacked, banned from cricket for a year and prevented from being captain for two. When Steve arrived back in Australia he held a press conference at the airport, and, with his dad's hand on his shoulder, burst into tears while apologizing: "I'll regret this for the rest of my life… I don't blame anyone. I'm the captain of the Australian team. It's on my watch and I take responsibility for what happened."

After a year out, Steve made his return in the World Cup and the Ashes tour that followed. He was the King of the Ashes, scoring 774 runs in the series, and was part of an epic battle with Jofra Archer at Lord's. He had to leave the field after being knocked down by a 92mph Archer bouncer that hit him on the neck. Ouch! He missed the next Test with concussion but returned at Old Trafford where he knocked together 211 and was cheered off the pitch. His career has been a rollercoaster, but he bats on, just pausing to fiddle and fiddle again between balls – a genius that can't stand still!

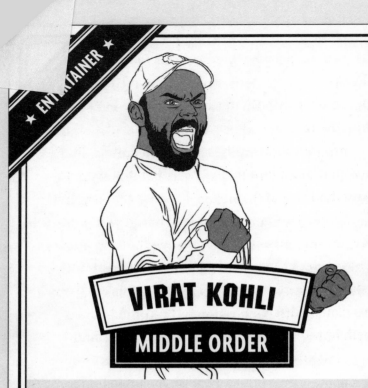

ENTERTAINER

VIRAT KOHLI

MIDDLE ORDER

COUNTRY: **INDIA**

CLUBS: **DELHI, ROYAL CHALLENGERS BANGALORE**

DATE OF BIRTH: **5 NOVEMBER 1988**

PLAYING STYLE: **RIGHT-HAND BAT**

NICKNAME: **CHIKU**

SUPERSTAR MOMENT: **MAKING TWO HUNDREDS AGAINST AUSTRALIA IN THE ADELAIDE TEST OF 2014**

FUN FACT: **THERE IS A CARTOON IN INDIA CALLED SUPER V, FEATURING AN ANIMATED VIRAT!**

VIRAT KOHLI

Did you know that Virat can drill holes in buildings with the force of his glare? OK, maybe only in his dreams, but Virat really, really likes to win. Luckily, he often does, as a member of the brilliant India team and one of the greatest batters in the world!

People thought that no one would ever replace Sachin Tendulkar as India's number one obsession. They were wrong. Virat, with his tattoos and his neatly cropped beard, his dreamy cover drive and his clenched fists, has roared the country along with him.

Virat is one of the best because he became a master of two things – technique and fitness. Traditionally, Indian batters were wonderful to watch at the crease but perhaps a little slow between the wickets. Not any more! Virat transformed himself and the team's attitude to fitness – running, lifting weights and doing Pilates. If you want to get in Virat's good books, get off the sofa and run to the nets. Now!

Virat grew up in Delhi, where he soon became the boy everyone was talking about. His dad, Prem, also loved the game but, sadly, Prem died when

Virat was eighteen. The morning after he died Virat carried on batting for Delhi – he couldn't bring himself to abandon the innings.

Virat was captain of the brilliant India side which won the U-19 World Cup in 2008 and was awarded a contract by IPL side Royal Challengers Bangalore when he was still a teenager. Aged nineteen, he was hauled into the India one-day team and made 50 in his fourth game, but floated in and out of the side. He was part of India's World Cup squad in 2011, making a hundred on his World Cup debut, against Bangladesh, and playing in every game including the final against Sri Lanka in Mumbai, which was watched by 997 million people worldwide. Imagine! Two years later, India won the Champions Trophy competition: Virat made vital runs in the semi-final and final. He was becoming the most awesome white-ball batter ever, and the man you wanted at the crease if you had to chase a big score. He loves the pressure of the chase.

Some people thought that Virat was too aggressive a batter and wouldn't take to Test cricket. Guess if he proved them wrong! There were struggles early on, especially in English conditions, but Virat worked and worked at his game and the hundreds started to flow, then the double-hundreds – he has seven, only Brian Lara, Don Bradman and Kumar Sangakkara have more. India lost the Border-Gavaskar Trophy of 2014–15, but Virat was supreme, making centuries in his first three innings as Test captain. He came back to England four years after his disastrous tour and made 593 magnificent Test runs. In a time when Test cricket is struggling for attention, Virat gives it a big hug. He calls it the purest form of the game, and says it has made him a better person because it's a "representation of life".

In 2020, the ICC named their teams of the decade. Guess who appeared in every format? Virat was also named male cricketer of the decade and ODI cricketer of the decade. He stepped down from the captaincy in January 2022, but not before leading India to their first Test series win in Australia. He's India's most successful Test captain ever!

AMELIA KERR

MIDDLE ORDER

COUNTRY: **NEW ZEALAND**

CLUBS: **WELLINGTON WOMEN, SOUTHERN BRAVE**

DATE OF BIRTH: **13 OCTOBER 2000**

PLAYING STYLE: **RIGHT-HAND BAT, RIGHT-ARM LEGSPIN**

NICKNAME: **MELIE**

SUPERSTAR MOMENT: **SCORING 232 IN 2018, THE HIGHEST SCORE IN WOMEN'S ODI HISTORY**

FUN FACT: **ALONGSIDE HER SPORTING CAREER, AMELIA IS ALSO STUDYING TO BECOME A TEACHER.**

AMELIA KERR

When you look at her family history, Amelia Kerr was always destined to become a cricketer. Her grandfather was a New Zealand international and so is her sister, Jess, while both of her parents played for Wellington. But Amelia is much more than just another cricketer in the Kerr family; she's an international cricket superstar and she has been since the age of seventeen!

In only her tenth ODI for New Zealand Amelia played an incredible innings that she will never forget, and neither will the poor Ireland bowlers she obliterated. That day in Dublin, she looked as comfortable and composed as an experienced pro as she batted her way through the full 50 overs, scoring an astonishing 232 runs off only 145 balls.

Yes, you read that right – 232 runs! "Blimey, must have been a real slog-fest!" you're probably thinking, but actually Amelia only scored two sixes in her entire innings. Instead, most of her runs came from fours – she hit 31 of them in fact – as she showed off her wide range of world-class shots all around the wicket. Although she didn't know it at the time, Amelia had just set a new women's

ODI highest score, beating the previous 21-year record by just three runs! She had also become the youngest-ever batter, male or female, to score a double-century in one-day cricket.

Woah! Amelia was suddenly a superstar, but she hasn't let the pressure get to her. She's now a key part of the New Zealand middle order, coming in after Amy Satterthwaite and her childhood hero Sophie Devine. What a brilliant batting line-up that is! And while she's yet to score another big century, Amelia did score a superb 72-not-out against England in 2021 (featuring an outrageous, over-the-head scoop shot for four) and a quick-fire 34 at the T20 World Cup against India. Plus, she's still so young that she's got years of brilliant batting ahead of her!

And bowling too. Want to know the most amazing thing of all about Amelia? People say she's actually a better bowler than a batter! In that same breakthrough game against Ireland she took five wickets for just seventeen runs, and since then she's become one of the best leg-spinners in the world.

With both bat and ball, Amelia is your perfect big-game player. She has "nerves of steel", according to New Zealand captain Sophie Devine. On her debut in Australia's Women's Big Bash League in 2019, Amelia bowled a triple-wicket maiden, and she also took a sensational hat-trick in the final of New Zealand's Super Smash T20 tournament in 2021. She was player of the series against India in early 2022 before the World Cup started on home soil. Unfortunately New Zealand were knocked out before she could really get going, but we know she's got so much more to achieve. Watch this space!

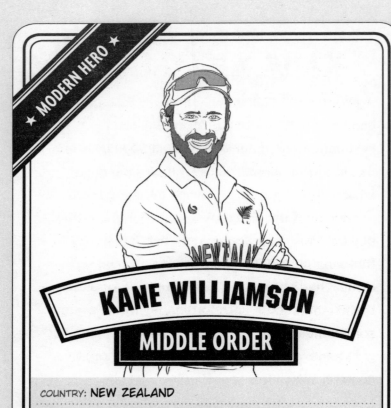

KANE WILLIAMSON

MIDDLE ORDER

COUNTRY: **NEW ZEALAND**

CLUBS: **NORTHERN DISTRICTS, SUNRISERS HYDERABAD, YORKSHIRE**

DATE OF BIRTH: **8 AUGUST 1990**

PLAYING STYLE: **RIGHT-HAND BAT**

NICKNAME: **STEADY THE SHIP**

SUPERSTAR MOMENT: **PLAYER OF THE TOURNAMENT IN THE 2019 WORLD CUP**

FUN FACT: **HE HAS A TWIN BROTHER CALLED LOGAN.**

KANE WILLIAMSON

Are you quiet? Shy? Do you think this means you can't be a cricketer? Meet Kane Williamson, the best batter to come from New Zealand, and the most modest, laid-back surfer dude to ever pick up a bat.

When Kane's parents went to fetch their little boy from his cot after a nap they watched him throw a mini ball into a hoop about three feet away. They were rather surprised – who can blame them! – but Kane's sporting success would be something they'd have to get used to.

Kane's older sisters played volleyball for New Zealand age-group teams and he and twin brother Logan were always outside playing sport alongside the neighbouring kids. Two – Trent Boult and Doug Bracewell – would go on to play for New Zealand, and another, Daniel Braid, would play for New Zealand's famous All Blacks rugby team. Pretty cool area to grow up in, huh?

Kane first pulled on his pads for Northern Districts at seventeen, making two and zero. On his one-day international debut, he also made a duck. But Kane was calm when he walked out in his first Test. The Indians were mad when he wasn't given out early on in the innings, and bowled furiously and at his body. But Kane just played every ball on its merits and casually notched up a hundred. Not a bad start to his Test career...

Twelve years on and he is still essentially the same player, with a perfect defence and no ego. Kane doesn't play outrageous made-up shots – oh no – he remains loyal to the coaching books, so correct, comfortable against spin or speed. His signature shot is a little dab to rotate the strike, and with soft hands, always soft hands. He is the same in all formats, from T20 to Tests. The theory is that he is so likeable and relaxed at the crease that the opposition kind of forget about him. Big mistake!

Look at his scores: a double-century against Sri Lanka to bring New Zealand from behind to win in 2015, and another against Bangladesh in 2019 to become the first New Zealander to ever make twenty Test centuries. One of the Fab Four world batters, he was the obvious choice as captain, and is just as quietly brilliant at that as he is at everything else. He soon led his New Zealand side (a country of just five million people) to a series of remarkable victories, away against England and Pakistan and all the way to winning the World Test Championship.

But perhaps his most famous moments have come during defeats. The 2019 World Cup final went down to a super over in nail-biting, crazy scenes at Lord's. When even the super over was a tie, England won because they'd hit more boundaries. While England celebrated, Kane was gallant and extraordinary in defeat.

Then two years later in the T20 World Cup final Kane played a real captain's innings of 85, but his New Zealand team were beaten again, this time by their big rivals Australia. "They are a brilliant side," Kane said graciously after the game, "and they thoroughly deserved it." We shouldn't be surprised. It's just the (fantastic) way he is.

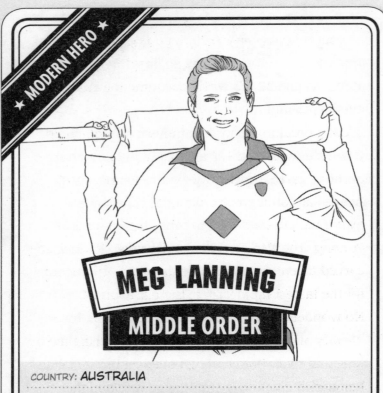

MEG LANNING

MIDDLE ORDER

COUNTRY: **AUSTRALIA**

CLUBS: **MELBOURNE STARS, VICTORIA**

DATE OF BIRTH: **25 MARCH 1992**

PLAYING STYLE: **RIGHT-HAND BAT**

NICKNAME: **MEGASTAR**

SUPERSTAR MOMENT: **LIFTING THE 2020 T20 WORLD CUP IN FRONT OF 86,000 PEOPLE AT THE MCG**

FUN FACT: **MEG IS A BIG FOODIE. WHEN ASKED WHICH FAMOUS PERSON SHE WOULD LIKE TO TRAVEL WITH, SHE CHOSE TV COOK NIGELLA LAWSON TO BE HER PRIVATE CHEF!**

MEG LANNING

Meg was just 21 when she became the youngest-ever captain of Australia, but by then she was used to breaking records! She was only eighteen when she walloped 103 not out in only her second one-day game, beating the record for youngest Australian to hit an international century held by her idol, ex-Australian men's captain Ricky Ponting. Then, in an ODI against New Zealand, she carved a century off 45 balls, breaking the record for the fastest hundred for an Australian woman. No wonder she is called "Megastar"!

Meg was born in Singapore and moved a few times as a kid. But wherever she went she took her cricket bag with her. She and her four sporty siblings played cricket in their backyard, but if they didn't hit straight back up the pitch they were in BIG trouble ... sending the ball square broke the windows! Meg became the first girl to play first XI cricket for a state school when she was fourteen; four years later she was playing for Australia!

Meg led Australia to their third consecutive T20 World Cup win in 2014, just after she was made captain, hitting 44 in the final. She also smashed

126 against Ireland in a group game – then the highest score in T20 women's internationals.

Her aggressive way of batting, hitting sixes for fun, has made her a hero, but almost more intimidating for opponents is the steely look in her eyes that she gets when she is annoyed. Meg hates getting out, and she hates losing!

She has led Australia to a record run in ODI and successive T20 World Cup victories. On 8 March 2020, she lifted the World Cup in front of 86,000 deliriously happy people at the Melbourne Cricket

Ground on International Women's Day, with pop star Katy Perry playing before and after the match. People couldn't believe how far women's cricket had come from the days when only a few hundred people would turn up to watch. Amazing! Meg and Australia did it again in the 2022 World Cup final, thrashing England by 71 runs to lift the trophy.

Meg is the leader of the greatest women's team in history – it is a dream come true.

JOE ROOT

MIDDLE ORDER

COUNTRY: **ENGLAND**

CLUBS: **YORKSHIRE, TRENT ROCKETS**

DATE OF BIRTH: **30 DECEMBER 1990**

PLAYING STYLE: **RIGHT-HAND BAT, OCCASIONAL SPINNER**

NICKNAME: **ROOTY**

SUPERSTAR MOMENT: **130 AGAINST AUSTRALIA AT TRENT BRIDGE WHICH HELPED WIN THE MATCH AND MADE HIM NO. 1 BATTER IN THE WORLD**

FUN FACT: **JOE'S FAVOURITE FOOTBALL TEAM IS SHEFFIELD UNITED. HE WAS THRILLED WHEN SOME OF THE PLAYERS SENT A VIDEO TO CONGRATULATE HIM ON HIS 100TH TEST APPEARANCE!**

JOE ROOT

One of the Fab Four batters in the world today, Joe shines out of the England batting line-up like a shooting star! For five years, he was also the Test captain, in charge of a team that could make you laugh or cry, sometimes in the same match. Yet Joe always seems to have a smile on his face.

Although he has been shuffled about the order a bit, Joe likes batting at number 4. He is unbelievably calm at the crease, and very graceful, as happy playing a cover-drive as a daring upper-cut. He is especially brilliant against spin, pleasing the commentators by getting properly forward and back to counter the turning ball. On the winter tours of 2020–21 he made 186 and 228 in Sri Lanka and then, in his 100th Test, 218 against India at Chennai.

Joe grew up in Sheffield, where he was always playing cricket with his grandad Don (named after Bradman), dad, Matt, and younger brother, Billy, who is a batter for Glamorgan. Joe was always good, and by the time he was playing for Yorkshire at nineteen, he was known as FEC, Future England Captain.

On his Test debut against India he didn't stop grinning for five days, and made a silky 73. Five matches later he hit his debut Test hundred against New Zealand at his home ground of Headingley, which made a lot of Yorkshire fans very happy! There was a hiccup a few weeks later when he had a 2 a.m. argument with David Warner in a Birmingham bar over a fake beard. Bad move! Warner threw a punch and was suspended. Joe, however, seemed unfazed and went on to make 180 against Australia at Lord's later that season as England won the Ashes. His brother Billy was twelfth man for that game and he was delighted to tell Joe how slowly he was batting, how boring he was being and that he could do better!

Joe suffered a slump in form during England's 2013–14 thrashing in the return Ashes series over in Australia and was dropped for the fifth Test. He worried that he would never play for England again – but in his comeback match the following summer he made an unbeaten 200!

The runs continued to flow and flow and, sure enough, he was made Test captain when Alastair Cook retired. Leading England is always a tricky job, especially during a pandemic, and after a good start the results started to go downhill, and Joe resigned in April 2022. There was always light relief though, as a member of England's one-day side, led by Eoin Morgan. There, he can just concentrate on his batting. He was England's highest run scorer in the 2019 50-over World Cup, and was part of the team that won the greatest final ever!

What a lot he has achieved! And at only 31, he's still in his cricketing prime.

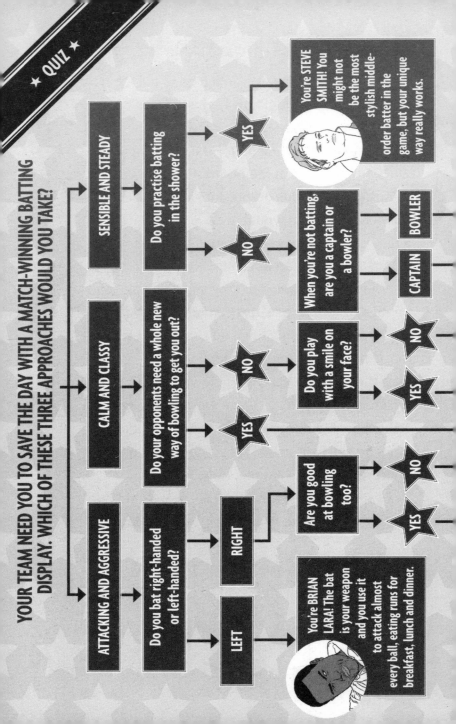

★ QUIZ ★

YOUR TEAM NEED YOU TO SAVE THE DAY WITH A MATCH-WINNING BATTING DISPLAY. WHICH OF THESE THREE APPROACHES WOULD YOU TAKE?

ATTACKING AND AGGRESSIVE

CALM AND CLASSY

SENSIBLE AND STEADY

Do you bat right-handed or left-handed?

Do your opponents need a whole new way of bowling to get you out?

Do you practise batting in the shower?

LEFT

RIGHT

YES

NO

YES

NO

You're BRIAN LARA! The bat is your weapon and you use it to attack almost every ball, eating runs for breakfast, lunch and dinner.

Are you good at bowling too?

Do you play with a smile on your face?

When you're not batting, are you a captain or a bowler?

YES

NO

YES

NO

CAPTAIN

BOWLER

You're STEVE SMITH! You might not be the most stylish middle-order batter in the game, but your unique way really works.

You're AMELIA KERR! As a great team player, you can hit a wide range of world-class shots and take lots of wickets too.

You're KANE WILLIAMSON! Absolutely nothing fazes you – not even scary fast bowlers or finding your team in trouble. You just calmly go out there and save the day, with your perfect defence, soft hands and classic shots.

You're SACHIN TENDULKAR! You're a middle-order run machine who has it all: perfect balance, beautiful timing and outrageous talent.

Are you a fitness fanatic?

YES **NO**

You're VIRAT KOHLI! Your batting technique is amazing, and so is your attitude. Pilates, weights or hours of practice in the nets – you'll do whatever it takes to win.

You're VIV RICHARDS! You're a formidable all-round athlete and when you're in the mood, you're one of the biggest hitters around.

You're MEG LANNING! You've got the skills and the aggression to hit the ball hard and far. You love lifting trophies and you can't stand losing!

You're DON BRADMAN! You're a batting genius who can do it all: defend or attack, play simple shots or stylish ones. Good luck to any bowlers trying to stop you!

You're JOE ROOT! You're a brilliant batter who can stay focused and keep the runs flowing for hours. And best of all, you enjoy every ball.

**3
ALL-
ROUNDERS**

ALL-ROUNDERS

Bat or bowl? That right there is the biggest question in cricket. Growing up, you usually get to do a bit of both before working out which one you're better at. But some still can't decide; they're equally brilliant at batting and bowling, and so they become ... all-rounders! So, what does it take to become an all-star all-rounder?

THREE THINGS ALL ALL-ROUNDERS MUST HAVE:

1 EXTRA LEVELS OF ENERGY Batting and bowling are two tiring activities, so doing both in the same game is doubly draining. All-rounder is an all-action role, so you'd better like being busy.

2 A MASSIVE DESIRE TO MAKE A DIFFERENCE When you bat and bowl, that means you get two attempts at being the hero for your team. So if you mess up once there's always a second chance to save the day. Hurray!

3 A REAL LOVE OF EVERYTHING CRICKET! Because all-rounders really can't get enough of the game.

THE BATTING-BOWLING BALANCE

A lot of cricketers get called "all-rounders" when they don't really deserve that title. Even most genuine all-rounders aren't equally good at both batting and bowling; most are world-class at one and also very good at the other. To explain, let's look at two South Africans who feature at either end of the all-rounder scale:

JACQUES KALLIS When you hear the stats, Kallis sounds like the ultimate all-rounder. He's still the only cricketer in the history of the game to score more than 10,000 runs and take over 250 wickets in both ODI and Test match cricket. But really, Kallis was always a much better batter than a bowler. While he's scored the third-highest number of runs in Test match history, he's way down in 37th on the list for most wickets.

SHAUN POLLOCK Pollock, meanwhile, sits up in twelfth on the wickets list, but he's nowhere to be seen on the batting chart. Although he was always known as an all-rounder, Pollock often came in at number 8 or 9 for South Africa. He even holds the record for playing the most ODI innings before scoring a century – 189!

INCREDIBLE INNOVATORS

In the thrilling new era of T20 cricket, the games are so short that players need to be more creative than ever. Batters are showing off all kinds of cool new shots, bowlers are using a range of clever new deliveries, and, in the field, **boundary catches** are getting more and more spectacular. And which players are the most inventive of all? Yes, you guessed it – those all-action all-rounders!

REVERSE SWEEP Go down on one knee as if you're going for the sweep, but this time flip your bat around and hit the ball in the opposite direction. A difficult shot to master, but worth it because it really annoys the bowler! All-rounder who plays it well: Glenn Maxwell, Australia.

PADDLE SCOOP Hold your bat down low in front of you and use it as a ramp to flick the ball backwards, up over the keeper's head. Very entertaining when it works; very embarrassing when it doesn't! All-rounder who plays it well: Hardik Pandya, India.

SWITCH HIT As the bowler runs in, quickly switch from batting with your stronger hand to batting with your weaker one. Why? Because it enables you to hit the ball into areas where there are fewer fielders. But warning: this takes a lot of practice! All-rounder who plays it well: Ben Stokes, England.

HELICOPTER SHOOT If a delivery is heading low towards your feet, use your wrists to flick the ball ferociously and allow your bat to follow through, doing a full circle over your head. All-rounder who plays it well: Rashid Khan, Afghanistan (NB he's in this book as a spinner, but he definitely thinks of himself as an all-rounder!).

CRICKET MADE EASY

"BOUNDARY CATCHES"

You're fielding out on the boundary and the ball is flying towards you. You know you can catch it, but you don't want to step over the boundary rope and give away a six. What should you do?

The most inventive and athletic modern cricketers have developed a clever way of leaping into the air, parrying the ball back the way it came, landing and then running back over the rope to complete the catch. "BOUNDARY CATCHES" are incredible!

ALL-ROUNDER RECORDS

Only six cricketers have ever scored 100 runs and taken ten wickets in a Test match:

BETTY WILSON
Australia v. England, 1958
(112r, 11w)

And he was playing with a broken finger!

ALAN DAVIDSON
Australia v. West Indies, 1960
(124r, 11w)

ENID BAKEWELL
England v. West Indies, 1979
(180r, 10w)

IAN BOTHAM
England v. India, 1980
(114r, 13w)

IMRAN KHAN
Pakistan v. India, 1983
(117r, 11w)

SHAKIB AL HASAN
Bangladesh v. Zimbabwe, 2014
(143r, 10w)

And only four cricketers have ever scored 100 runs and taken five or more wickets in a one-day international match:

VIV RICHARDS
West Indies v. New Zealand, 1987
(119r, 5w)

PAUL COLLINGWOOD
England v. Bangladesh, 2005
(112r, 6w)

ROHAN MUSTAFA
UAE v. Papua New Guinea, 2017
(109r, 5w)

AMELIA KERR
New Zealand v. Ireland, 2018
(232r, 5w)

SO, WHICH KIND OF ALL-ROUNDER WOULD YOU BE?

You see, it takes a very special cricketer to be equally good at both, but here's a look at eight all-rounders, past and present, who we can definitely call superstars with bat and ball. Then take the quiz at the end to find out which of these amazing players you would be.

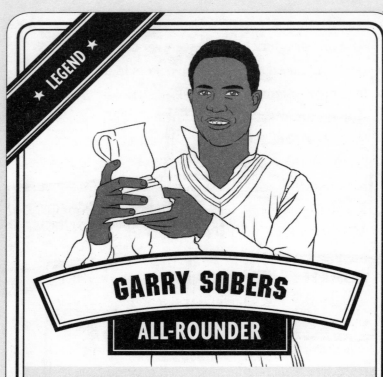

GARRY SOBERS

ALL-ROUNDER

COUNTRY: **WEST INDIES**

CLUBS: **BARBADOS, NOTTINGHAMSHIRE**

DATE OF BIRTH: **28 JULY 1936**

PLAYING STYLE: **LEFT-HAND BAT, LEFT-ARM FAST MEDIUM AND LEFT-ARM SPIN**

NICKNAME: **KING CRICKET**

SUPERSTAR MOMENT: **SETTING A NEW BATTING WORLD RECORD BY SCORING 365 AGAINST PAKISTAN IN 1958**

FUN FACT: **HE HAS A FAMOUS SONG WRITTEN ABOUT HIM - "SIR GARFIELD SOBERS" BY MIGHTY SPARROW.**

GARRY SOBERS

It's only right that we start this section with the story of Garry (real name Garfield) Sobers, the greatest all-rounder to ever play the game. "Genius" is a word that people use a lot, but when it comes to Sobers and cricket it seems entirely accurate. As a batter he was one of the best in history, scoring 26 Test centuries and averaging 57.78 runs per innings. He was a world-class bowler too, taking 235 wickets with a combination of pace and spin, and he was also a fantastic fielder. Don Bradman himself even once described Sobers as a "five-in-one cricketer".

Garry grew up playing cricket on the island of Barbados and, aged just seventeen, he made his international debut for the West Indies against England. For his first Test, Garry was mainly used as a bowler, and he showed his talent by taking four wickets. But surely he was too good with the bat to be a lowly number 9? When Garry played his next match a year later he had been moved up the order to 6 – much better! He went on to score 231 runs in the series against Australia – see, he wasn't just a bowler; he was an amazing all-rounder!

Garry's batting got better and better, but it was still a bit of a surprise when, at the age of 21, he set a new Test record in 1958 by scoring 365 not out against Pakistan. What an astonishing performance – before that, his highest score had been 80! And Garry was no one-innings wonder; he followed that up with two more centuries in a row.

Right, on to the next big challenge – could Garry bat and bowl brilliantly at the same time? Of course he could! When the West Indies toured Australia in 1960 he took fifteen wickets and twelve catches, as well as scoring 430 runs. What a multi-talented man! From that moment onwards, Garry became the greatest all-rounder in the game, winning the "Wisden Leading Cricketer in the World" title eight times in thirteen years, and twice scoring a century and taking five wickets in the same innings. In 1965, he led the West Indies to their first-ever Test series victory over Australia, and a year later, he played so well against England that people started calling him "King Cricket"!

At the peak of his powers in the 1960s, Garry was such a great all-rounder that he could do absolutely anything. He would sometimes even bowl fast, medium pace and two types of spin, all in the same Test! Often it seemed like the game of cricket was just too easy for him, as if he could play it in his sleep. The story goes that during a match in 1968, he was having a nap in the dressing room when a teammate woke him suddenly and said, "You're in!" Up Garry got and out he went to score 132, before returning to the dressing room for the rest of his nap!

He was a born entertainer, and while he never quite matched his magical 365 against Pakistan, Garry did set one other unbelievable batting record. In 1968, while playing for English club Nottinghamshire, he became the first cricketer ever to score six sixes in one over! Just imagine being Malcolm Nash, the poor bowler who had to watch as his deliveries sailed high into the crowd again and again. Garry hit the last ball so hard that it landed in a nearby garden. Luckily, a young boy named Richard Lewis managed to find it and give it back to Garry afterwards.

So there you have it – the short story of the greatest all-rounder to ever play the game. In 1975, the Queen knighted him Sir Garry Sobers, but he'll always be "King Cricket" to us.

IMRAN KHAN
ALL-ROUNDER

COUNTRY: **PAKISTAN**

CLUB: **LAHORE**

DATE OF BIRTH: **5 OCTOBER 1952**

PLAYING STYLE: **RIGHT-HAND BAT, RIGHT-ARM FAST BOWLER**

NICKNAME: **THE LION OF LAHORE**

SUPERSTAR MOMENT: **CAPTAINING PAKISTAN TO VICTORY IN THE 1992 WORLD CUP**

FUN FACT: **IMRAN SEEMS TO HAVE TWO BIRTHDAYS. SOME SAY IT'S 5 OCTOBER, SOME SAY IT'S 25 NOVEMBER.**

LEGEND

IMRAN KHAN

Even for an all-rounder, Imran Khan is a man of
many talents – batting, bowling, writing, leading
his national cricket team, and leading his entire
country too. Yes, in 2018, he became the Prime
Minister of Pakistan! But this is a book about
cricket, not politics, so let's go back and look at his
incredible international career with bat and ball,
which lasted 21 years.

Imran made his Test debut for Pakistan against
England in 1971 at the age of just eighteen. Wow,
can you imagine the pressure on someone so
young?! So it's no surprise that his match stats
were pretty poor – five runs and zero wickets –
and sadly he didn't play for his country again for
three years. But Imran the cricketer was only just
getting started. As a batter he developed a solid
defensive style and then began to build bigger
and better innings until he scored his first Test
century for Pakistan against the West Indies in
1980. Slowly but surely he moved his way up the
batting order: from 8 to 7, and then to 6, where he
shone brightest. In fact, only one player in history
has a better average at number 6 and that's West

Indian Shivnarine Chanderpaul, an out-and-out batter.

As Imran got older he also improved as a bowler. Back in that first Test against England, he was still only medium-pace, but through hard work and a change of action he turned himself into one of the fastest in the world. The third-fastest, in fact, according to a special bowling contest in 1978, where he finished behind Jeff Thomson of Australia and Michael Holding of the West Indies (more about him later in the book). And speed wasn't Imran's only weapon as a bowler; he also became the first king of reverse-swing. With so many different ways to get a batter out, Imran was almost unbeatable at his peak in 1982. He took 62 wickets in total, including fourteen in a single Test against Sri Lanka, and then another 21 in a three-match series against England (where he also scored 212 runs).

With amazing all-round stats like that, Imran seemed like the perfect player to be the new Pakistan cricket captain. And what a wise choice he was! He soon showed that leadership was, in fact, his greatest strength of all. The extra responsibility only seemed to make him even better as a batter and a bowler. With Imran in charge, Pakistan recorded their first-ever series wins away in India and England, and also drew with the mighty West Indies.

Imran's greatest moment, however, as both a cricketer and a captain, came in the 1992 World Cup. By then he was 39 years old and more of a batter than a bowler, but he still had the all-round skill and strength of character to lead Pakistan to their first, and so far only, international trophy. First, Imran came in at number 3 and scored a steady 72 to help set England a target of 250 to chase. Then, once Wasim Akram (one of the new reverse-swing kings, taught by Imran) had done most of the damage with the ball it was the captain himself who took the final wicket to win the game. Pakistan were the World Cup winners! With his arms raised above his head like a hero, Imran led his team on a lap of honour around the pitch.

What a way to wave goodbye to international cricket! Imran didn't stay retired for too long, though; soon, a second career in politics was calling...

BEN STOKES

ALL-ROUNDER

COUNTRY: **ENGLAND**

CLUBS: **DURHAM, RAJASTHAN ROYALS**

DATE OF BIRTH: **4 JUNE 1991**

PLAYING STYLE: **LEFT-HAND BAT, RIGHT-ARM FAST-MEDIUM**

NICKNAME: **MR INCREDIBLE**

SUPERSTAR MOMENT: **BATTING ENGLAND TO VICTORY IN THE 2019 CRICKET WORLD CUP FINAL**

FUN FACT: **BEN HAS HIS ENGLAND TEST NUMBER, ODI NUMBER AND T20 NUMBER TATTOOED ON HIS ARMS. OUCH!**

BEN STOKES

Say "Hi!" to England's new Test captain! Yes, Ben Stokes, the man who can do everything, has a new job. He took over from Joe Root in April 2022 – so it's lucky he has a lot of energy! Mr Incredible, as he is nicknamed, is an all-rounder who knows all about the ups and downs of cricket and what it takes to become a game-changing superstar.

Ben was born in New Zealand, where his dad, Ged, was a Rugby League player, but cricket was the sport that he fell in love with, and England was the country that he chose to represent. That's where his mum, Debbie, is from, and the Stokes family moved back there when Ben was twelve. Five years later he made his first-team debut for Durham, bowling out one of England's best batters, Mark Ramprakash, with only his third delivery, before hitting the winning runs himself!

The boy wonder had it all – talent, aggression, and tons of self-belief. Surely Ben was a future England superstar? But first he needed to prove himself in county cricket. In 2013, he scored 615 runs and took 42 wickets as Durham won the County Championship, and a year later he was

 named the Player of the Match in the One-Day Cup final at Lord's. So, was Ben now ready to shine for England on the world stage? At first, there were moments of magic – 5–61 in an ODI against Australia, 258 runs off 198 balls in a Test against South Africa – but also frustrating failures. After a poor run of form he was left out of England's squad for the 2015 Cricket World Cup, and then in the 2016 T20 World Cup final he bowled a bad final over to hand victory to the West Indies. Noooo!

As well as those disappointments there were also some bad decisions along the way. Ben was once sent home from an England Lions tour for bad behaviour, he missed the 2014 World Twenty20 with a broken wrist after punching a locker in anger, and in 2017 he was banned for eight matches after getting into a fight.

By 2019, however, Ben had learned his lessons and he was determined to bounce back in style with both bat and ball. He wanted to show everyone what an amazing all-rounder he really was, so he powered England all the way to the Cricket World Cup final, and then pulled out his best performance in the biggest game of all, against his birth country, New Zealand. When Ben came in to bat, England were struggling at 71–3, chasing 242 to win. Usually he likes to play lots of powerful, aggressive shots, but that wasn't what his team needed at that moment. They needed a cool-headed hero, and so Ben adapted his game and scored a slower, steadier 84-not-out instead.

At the end of their 50 overs, however, England finished on 241 runs, the exact same score as New Zealand. So, the match went to a super over, and who did England send out to bat for them? Ben, of course! They needed his power and his calm under pressure. Using every last scrap of his strength and energy he went back out and scored 15 runs with his partner, Jos Buttler. New Zealand

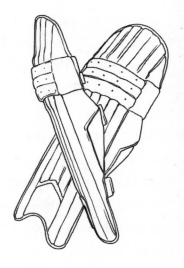

couldn't beat that, which meant England were
the winners, the Cricket Champions of the World!
Ben threw himself down on the grass, emotional
and exhausted. Despite all the setbacks and
disappointments, he had done it – he had become
England's hero!

And just six weeks later Ben did it again during the Ashes series against Australia. On the final day of the third Test England were desperately attempting to avoid another defeat. But while wickets fell around him Ben stayed strong and focused, batting on and on, past 50 and then past 100. He should have been tired after a long and brilliant spell of bowling the previous day, but he certainly didn't show it. As hard as they tried, Australia just couldn't get Ben out, and thanks to an astonishing last-wicket partnership with Jack Leach he somehow led England all the way to victory! It was the second miracle of the summer from one of cricket's most magical superstars.

STAFANIE TAYLOR

ALL-ROUNDER

COUNTRY: **WEST INDIES**

CLUBS: **JAMAICA, ADELAIDE STRIKERS, SOUTHERN BRAVE**

DATE OF BIRTH: **11 JUNE 1991**

PLAYING STYLE: **RIGHT-HAND BAT, RIGHT-HAND OFF-SPIN**

NICKNAME: **GWEN**

SUPERSTAR MOMENT: **LEADING THE WEST INDIES TO THE ICC WOMEN'S T20 WORLD CUP TITLE IN 2016**

FUN FACT: **SHE HAS A PASSION FOR FORENSIC SCIENCE (LOOKING AT DEAD BODIES AND STUFF LIKE THAT) AND WOULD LOVE TO ONE DAY BECOME A CRIME SCENE INVESTIGATOR.**

STAFANIE TAYLOR

Football or cricket? It's a difficult decision that lots of sporty kids have to make. Growing up on the island of Jamaica, Stafanie Taylor was one of the best young players at both, but in the end she chose cricket. Why? Because she thought it would give her a better chance to travel the world, and because she had the skills to become a superstar. Whether she was facing boys or girls, it didn't bother her; she always played the game with supreme confidence and zero fear. That's why her youth coach, Leon Campbell, used to tell her, "You are going to be the number one female cricketer in the world."

And it didn't take long for her to show off her special talent. At the age of seventeen, Stafanie made her T20I debut for the West Indies and blasted 90 runs off only 49 balls. It was an innings that her cricketing hero, Chris Gayle, would have been very proud of. Woah, this wonderkid could really bat! And she soon showed that she could really bowl too. After starting out as a fast bowler she switched to off-spin, and her slow, looping deliveries have caught out batter after batter. In

2009, Stafanie became the West Indies' top run-scorer and wicket-taker at both the Women's Cricket World Cup and the ICC Women's World Twenty20. Now, that's what we call an awesome all-rounder!

And that was just the start for Stafanie. At nineteen, she became the youngest woman ever to reach 1,000 ODI runs, and her batting scores kept getting better and better: 108 against South Africa, then 147 against the Netherlands, then a sensational 171 against Sri Lanka at the 2013 World Cup! Her bowling figures were brilliant too, and by 2014 she already had over 100 ODI wickets.

Stafanie won the ICC Women's Cricketer of the Year award in 2011, but her ultimate all-rounder achievement actually came two years later against New Zealand. First, she batted her way to a huge 135-not-out (her fourth century) and then she bowled her way to four wickets, becoming the first female cricketer to do that double in ODI history.

As she says herself, Stafanie isn't really a stats person; she's all about winning and so her proudest moment would have to be the 2016 Women's T20 World Cup. By then she was the new West Indies captain and she led by example, hitting the most runs in the whole tournament. Her lowest score was 25 and, like all great superstars, she saved her best until last. In the final against Australia, Stafanie scored 59 in a match-winning partnership with Hayley Matthews, a young all-rounder aiming to become "the next Stafanie Taylor". The West Indies Women were the World Champions for the first time ever! As well as the honour of lifting the trophy, Stafanie also collected the Player of the Tournament prize.

Since then, Stafanie's cricketing success has continued. In 2017, she became the fourth-fastest female to score 4,000 ODI runs, while in 2020 she became only the second woman ever to reach 3,000 T20I runs. When Stafanie stars, the West Indies win; it's as simple as that.

RECORD-BREAKER

ELLYSE PERRY
ALL-ROUNDER

COUNTRY: **AUSTRALIA**

CLUBS: **NEW SOUTH WALES, SYDNEY SIXERS, BIRMINGHAM PHOENIX**

DATE OF BIRTH: **3 NOVEMBER 1990**

PLAYING STYLE: **RIGHT-HAND BAT, RIGHT-ARM FAST-MEDIUM**

NICKNAME: **PEZ**

SUPERSTAR MOMENT: **WINNING THE 2013 CRICKET WORLD CUP WITH AUSTRALIA**

FUN FACT: **BETWEEN THE AGES OF 9 AND 23, ELLYSE KEPT THE SAME PAIR OF LUCKY SPORTS SOCKS!**

ELLYSE PERRY

Australia's Ellyse Perry is one of the true greats of the game – a record-breaking batter and bowler, and a five-time T20 World Cup winner. She's such an amazing all-rounder that she has played football, as well as cricket, for her country. In fact, she made her international debuts in both sports in the same year – 2007, before she had even celebrated her seventeenth birthday!

On the football pitch, Ellyse scored in an 8–1 win over Hong Kong (despite being a defender), while on the cricket pitch she grabbed two wickets and nineteen runs. Two promising debuts – so which sport did she prefer? Well, for a long time Ellyse just kept playing both. She starred for Australia at the 2011 FIFA Women's World Cup in Germany (check out her wondergoal against Sweden!) and also the 2013 ICC Women's Cricket World Cup in India. It was only a year later that her coaches forced her to choose and she chose ... CRICKET, of course!

In the end, it was an easy and obvious decision. As a footballer, Ellyse was good but as a cricketer, she's truly great. At first she was seen mainly as a fast, swing bowler – the perfect replacement for Australia's retiring legend Cathryn Fitzpatrick. But on her T20I debut in 2008 against England, Ellyse showed she could do everything. She started by scoring 29 off 25 balls, including a brilliant six, and then bowled beautifully, finishing with figures of 4–20. Oh, and Ellyse even showed off her fantastic fielding too by running Claire Taylor out, and she was still only eighteen years old! There was no doubt about it – she was going to be Australia's next great all-rounder.

Perhaps Ellyse's best quality of all, however, is that she's a real big-game player. She picked up the "Player of the Final" award at the World Twenty20 in 2010, and she was just as vital to Australia's victories in 2012, 2014 and 2018 too.

Another amazing all-round Ellyse performance came in the 2013 Cricket World Cup final where she scored a quick-fire 25-not-out with the bat and then took three wickets for nineteen with the ball, despite bowling with a bad ankle injury. What a warrior and a winner!

These days, Ellyse is one of the senior players in the Australia team, but she continues to work hard on her fitness and technique. As a bowler she's still one of the best in the world, and in 2019 she became only the third player ever to claim 150 ODI wickets. As a batter, Ellyse has got better and better with age, even moving up into the middle order. During the 2017–18 Women's Ashes series she hit a spectacular 213-not-out, the third-highest score in the history of women's Test cricket, and the highest by an Australian. And as an all-rounder, she became the first female player to reach 1,000 runs and 100 wickets in T20Is.

In 2020, Ellyse was named the ICC's greatest women's cricketer of the decade, and in 2022 she won the World Cup again with Australia. England star Charlotte Edwards went even further, calling her "the greatest female player we're ever going to see."

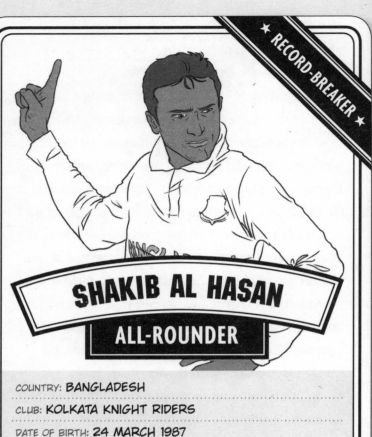

SHAKIB AL HASAN

ALL-ROUNDER

COUNTRY: **BANGLADESH**

CLUB: **KOLKATA KNIGHT RIDERS**

DATE OF BIRTH: **24 MARCH 1987**

PLAYING STYLE: **LEFT-HAND BAT, SLOW LEFT-ARM ORTHODOX SPIN**

NICKNAME: **MOYNA**

SUPERSTAR MOMENT: **BECOMING THE TOP-RANKED ALL-ROUNDER IN TEST, ODI AND T20I!**

FUN FACT: **IN 2010, SHAKIB JOINED WORCESTERSHIRE CRICKET CLUB, BECOMING THE FIRST BANGLADESHI EVER TO PLAY FOR AN ENGLISH COUNTY TEAM.**

SHAKIB AL HASAN

Despite Ben Stokes' match-winning moments, the award for best all-rounder in modern cricket must go to Bangladesh's Shakib Al Hasan. He's so good with both bat and ball that it doesn't matter what format he's playing.

Even as a youngster it was clear that Shakib was a special player. In 2005, he led the Bangladesh U-19s to victory against Sri Lanka in a tournament final, scoring a century off 86 balls and then taking three wickets too. Just a year after that amazing all-round performance Shakib was making his debut for his country's senior side.

At first, Shakib was seen as a better batter than a bowler, especially following his impressive performance at the 2007 Cricket World Cup. After a superb century against Canada he then hit two important 50s – one in a defeat to England, and the other in a shock win over India. Bangladesh had a new middle-order hero.

However, Shakib soon showed that his bowling was just as brilliant as his batting. Later that same year at the World T20 he took 4–34 to beat the West Indies, and then in 2008 he took seven wickets for 36 runs in a Test match against New Zealand. The batters just couldn't cope with his clever and consistent spin bowling.

By 2009 Shakib was already the top-ranked ODI all-rounder in the world, as well as the Bangladesh vice-captain. In the middle of a Test series against the West Indies, however, their captain, Mashrafe Mortaza, got injured, and so at the young age of 22 Shakib took over. Not only did he lead his team to victory in the first Test, but he also led them to victory in the second, taking eight wickets with the ball and scoring 96 not out with the bat. Thanks to their all-round superstar, Bangladesh had won their first-ever overseas Test series after nearly ten years of trying!

Shakib was named Test Player of the Year in 2009, and by 2011 he was also the top-ranked Test all-rounder in the world. ODI? Tick! Test? Tick! Now for T20s... Not many players have the talent to be equally incredible at every kind of cricket, but Shakib does. In 2012, he helped Kolkata Knight Riders win the IPL title, as well as smashing 84 off 54 balls in a T20I against Pakistan. By 2014, he had achieved his target – he was the top-ranked all-rounder in all three formats.

And Shakib didn't stop there. In a Test match against New Zealand in 2017, he hit a career-best of 217 and then he became one of the biggest stars of the 2019 Cricket World Cup. He scored 75 to help Bangladesh beat South Africa, then 121 against England, 124 against the West Indies, and best of all, against Afghanistan, he became only the second player ever to do the all-rounder double in a World Cup match – 50 runs and five wickets.

As you've seen, Shakib is an all-round superstar on the field, but off it, sadly his behaviour has not always been the best. In 2014, he was banned for eight months because of a "severe attitude problem, which is unprecedented in the history of Bangladesh cricket". And Shakib was given an even greater punishment in October 2019, just weeks after his wonderful World Cup performance. The ICC suspended him for a whole year for failing to report text messages he had received about match-fixing. Shakib apologized to his nation of fans, and now after serving his ban he's back doing what he does best – scoring runs and taking wickets. In fact, in 2021, he broke another record, becoming the leading wicket-taker in the history of men's T20 international cricket.

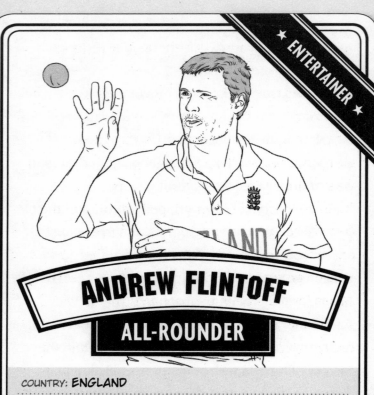

ANDREW FLINTOFF

ALL-ROUNDER

COUNTRY: **ENGLAND**

CLUB: **LANCASHIRE**

DATE OF BIRTH: **6 DECEMBER 1977**

PLAYING STYLE: **RIGHT-HAND BAT, RIGHT-ARM FAST-MEDIUM BOWLER**

NICKNAME: **FREDDIE**

SUPERSTAR MOMENT: **THE ENTIRE 2005 ASHES SERIES!**

FUN FACT: **ANDREW WAS A CHESS CHAMPION AT SCHOOL.**

ANDREW FLINTOFF

Earlier this century, before you were born, a cricket series captured the English imagination like no other. And during that series, one six-foot-four all-rounder was a hero amongst giants – that man was Andrew "Freddie" Flintoff.

In 2005, cricket fever gripped the UK and the country became obsessed as the series swung first one way, then the other. There were huge queues outside grounds, as England tried to win back the Ashes for the first time in eighteen years!

Freddie was at the peak of his powers, a hard-hitting biff-bash batter and a fast bowler who had the gift of making things happen. Charging in, he drew energy from the crowd who in turn roared him on. It was electrifying! He took 24 wickets that magical series, and scored 402 runs including a cracking hundred at Trent Bridge.

There is a famous picture taken at Edgbaston, at the end of the "greatest Test" of the greatest series. It shows Freddie with his arm around Brett Lee, the not-out batter stranded as England took the last wicket with Australia just two runs away from victory. Freddie had made two 50s, taken seven wickets and bowled one of the best overs ever, full of balls reverse-swinging at 90mph, but he still remembered what it was like to be on the losing side. What a hero!

The series was up in the air until the final afternoon of the final Test at The Oval. England won the series 2–1, and the country went bonkers as the team did an open-top bus tour of London and went to 10 Downing Street to meet the prime minister.

That was the beginning of the end of Freddie's golden period, as various bits of his body started complaining about the workload. Ouch! Standing in for the injured Michael Vaughan, he was appointed captain for the Ashes tour of 2006–07, but it all went horribly wrong. Whereas in 2005 he had the golden touch, now he had the opposite. England were thrashed, losing the series 5–0. Freddie's winter got even worse during the disappointing World Cup campaign that followed: he made a drunken decision to go out in a pedalo at 1.30 a.m. Not a good idea! He capsized and had to be rescued from the rough waters of the Caribbean Sea.

He had time for one more memorable summer, in 2009. He said goodbye to Lord's with five wickets, and then in the final Test of the summer he ran out Australian captain Ricky Ponting with a pin-point throw as England reclaimed the Ashes.

Since then, Freddie has had a go at being a boxer, then became a reality TV star and made important programmes about mental health. But you should remember him in his pomp, that golden summer, turning cricket into magic with bat and ball.

HARMANPREET KAUR

ALL-ROUNDER

COUNTRY: **INDIA**

CLUBS: **PUNJAB WOMEN, LANCASHIRE THUNDER, SYDNEY THUNDER, MANCHESTER ORIGINALS**

DATE OF BIRTH: **8 MARCH 1989**

PLAYING STYLE: **RIGHT-HAND BAT, RIGHT-ARM OFF-SPIN BOWLER**

NICKNAME: **HARMAN**

SUPERSTAR MOMENT: **HER 171-NOT-OUT TO BEAT AUSTRALIA IN THE SEMI-FINAL OF THE 2017 WOMEN'S WORLD CUP**

FUN FACT: **A LETTER FROM SACHIN TENDULKAR HELPED GET HARMANPREET A JOB!**

HARMANPREET KAUR

Harmanpreet exploded onto the international cricket stage with her 171-not-out in the semi-final of the 2017 Women's World Cup. It was an innings to blow minds and smash stereotypes. If anyone had slept through the early rounds, they were awake now! The innings was talked about EVERYWHERE!

The Australian team, who were on the receiving end of her huge hits, just looked bewildered, there was nothing they could do to stop her. Smashed off just 115 balls and including seven mega sixes, it had superstars such as Virat Kohli and Charlotte Edwards wide-eyed in delight.

She made a 50 in the final too, which India lost to England by nine runs, but it was Harmanpreet's 171 that caught the imagination. People said that it was as important to women's cricket in India as the 1983 Men's World Cup win had been to popularizing men's cricket. Nice one, Harmanpreet! How do you top that?!

Actually, Harmanpreet had been doing big things since she made her international debut in 2009, with her century against England in the 2013 World Cup, setting her career alight.

At just five foot three, Harmanpreet generates her incredible power with timing, with dancing feet and that bat swing. Have you seen her bat swing? She starts with the bat high in the air as if she were trying to tickle an elephant's armpit, and finishes with a huge follow-through like a golfer. Warning: don't try it out in your kitchen! She was the first Indian cricketer to earn an overseas T20 contract

with Sydney Thunder, and is also a handy part-time spinner, taking important wickets when the main bowlers struggle.

She led India's T20 team to the final of the World Cup in Australia in 2020. They lost to Australia, but their day will come, inspired by Harmanpreet, their fearless captain fantastic!

YOU'RE BRILLIANT AT BOTH BATTING AND BOWLING, BUT IF YOU COULD ONLY CHOOSE ONE, WHICH ARE YOU BETTER AT?

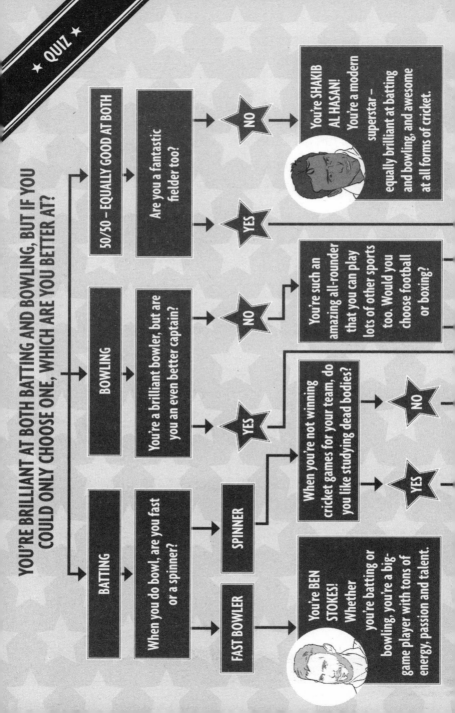

BATTING

When you do bowl, are you fast or a spinner?

FAST BOWLER

SPINNER

You're BEN STOKES! Whether you're batting or bowling, you're a big-game player with tons of energy, passion and talent.

When you're not winning cricket games for your team, do you like studying dead bodies?

YES

NO

BOWLING

You're a brilliant bowler, but are you an even better captain?

YES

NO

You're such an amazing all-rounder that you can play lots of other sports too. Would you choose football or boxing?

50/50 – EQUALLY GOOD AT BOTH

Are you a fantastic fielder too?

YES

NO

You're SHAKIB AL HASAN! You're a modern superstar – equally brilliant at batting and bowling, and awesome at all forms of cricket.

You're GARRY SOBERS! You're the complete package and people will be calling you "King Cricket" in years to come.

BOXING

FOOTBALL

You're ANDREW FLINTOFF! Being big and strong helps you to bowl the ball fast and hit the ball hard. Yes, boxing is much more physical than cricket, but you're up for any challenge!

You're ELLYSE PERRY! You've got the fitness, focus and ball skills to be good at any sport, but when it comes to cricket, you're a star! Whether you're batting, bowling or fielding, you're a warrior and a winner.

You're STAFANIE TAYLOR! You're a born leader, an awesome all-rounder and you're not afraid of anything.

You're HARMANPREET KAUR! Your bowling is good, but your batting is GREAT. With one big swing, you can send the ball flying through the sky for six.

You're IMRAN KHAN! You love to lead by example with bat and ball, inspiring your team to victory. And when your cricketing days are over, who knows, maybe you'll have a second career in politics.

4

WICKET-
KEEPERS

WICKET-KEEPERS

In the last section we talked about the importance of fielding if you want to become a true all-rounder. But if you really, really love taking incredible catches and running people out, then why not become a wicket-keeper?

THREE THINGS ALL WICKET-KEEPERS MUST HAVE:

1 EXCELLENT EYESIGHT Standing (or crouching) behind the stumps, it's your job to stop every ball that flies past the bat, however high or wide it might be, and however much it spins or swings. And if it hits the edge of the bat, then you don't just need to stop it; you need to catch it.

2 CAT-LIKE REFLEXES Sometimes, a wicket-keeper might take a simple catch while standing still, but most of the time they're on the move. And don't expect much warning about where the ball is going to go; just be ready to react in a flash for the chance of a catch or **stumping**.

3 A HARD AND SAFE PAIR OF HANDS! Because catching super-fast balls can really start to hurt after a while.

THE "STUMPING"

A wicket-keeper has three* ways to get a batter out:

- A CATCH
- A RUN-OUT
- A "STUMPING"

"STUMPING" doesn't mean confusing them with riddles or tricky quiz questions, although a lot of wicket-keepers do like to talk all day long. No, it's when a batter comes forward out of their crease for a big hit but misses the ball, and the wicket-keeper catches it and whips off the bails in a flash before the batter can get back in. OUT! This mostly only happens with slower spin bowling because that's when the wicket-keeper can safely stand up close to the stumps. It requires fast and very skilful glovework, but if you get it right, it's a glorious feeling!

*Well, four if you include appealing for LBW (leg before wicket) so loudly that the umpire gives it.

GREAT WITH THE GLOVES

In the old days, wicket-keeper was a cricket position of its own. Often, players were picked purely for their skills behind the stumps, and if they were also really handy with the bat, well, that was just a nice bonus. Australian Bert Oldfield was known as the first great wicket-keeper, but he only averaged 22 with the bat and his highest-ever score in 80 Test match innings was 65 not out. Jeff Dujon, meanwhile, the best glovesman of the 1980s, often batted way down at number 8 for the West Indies. Even the mighty Mark Boucher averaged fewer than 30 runs per innings in one-day cricket.

But these guys weren't in the team for their batting; they were in the team for their catching, keeping and organizational skills. You see, from behind the stumps the wicket-keeper has the best view of the game and touches the ball more than most other players. So, part of the role is to pass on information and encourage everyone around them – the bowler, the fielders – except for the batters, of course!

BRILLIANT WITH THE BAT, TOO

By the late 1990s, however, the game had started to change. With teams trying to score lots of runs quickly, especially in one-day cricket, it made sense to have as many big-hitters in the line-up as possible. Yes, you still wanted wicket-keepers who were great with the gloves, but they now had to be brilliant with the bat too. Two positions for the price of one!

The era of the wicket-keeper batter began with Australia's Adam Gilchrist. "Gilly" was very good behind the stumps, but he was even better in front of them. In fact, he was so good that he opened the batting for his country in one-day cricket and scored nearly 4,000 runs at number 7 in Test matches. Gilchrist paved the way, and since then the likes of Kumar Sangakkara, MS Dhoni, AB de Villiers, Jos Buttler and now Rishabh Pant have all followed in his multi-talented footsteps.

WICKET-KEEPER RECORDS

Here's a look at the greatest of all time with the gloves:

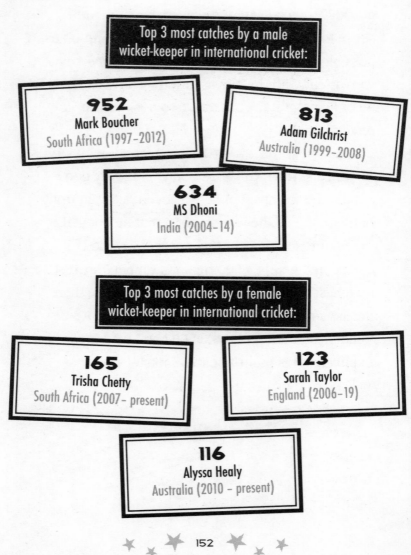

Top 3 most catches by a male wicket-keeper in international cricket:

952
Mark Boucher
South Africa (1997–2012)

813
Adam Gilchrist
Australia (1999–2008)

634
MS Dhoni
India (2004–14)

Top 3 most catches by a female wicket-keeper in international cricket:

165
Trisha Chetty
South Africa (2007– present)

123
Sarah Taylor
England (2006–19)

116
Alyssa Healy
Australia (2010 – present)

SO, WHICH KIND OF WICKET-KEEPER WOULD YOU BE?

Would you be a wicket-keeper first, or better with the bat? Would you be an explosive opener, or a solid number 7? Which would you care more about: catches or centuries? To help you decide, here's a range of wonderful wicket-keepers for you to read all about. Then take the quiz at the end to find out which of these superstars you would be.

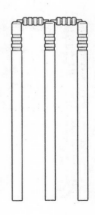

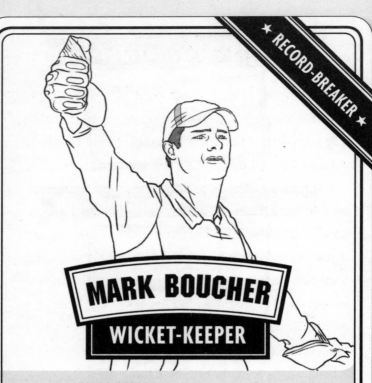

MARK BOUCHER
WICKET-KEEPER

COUNTRY: **SOUTH AFRICA**

CLUBS: **BORDER, THE WARRIORS**

DATE OF BIRTH: **3 DECEMBER 1976**

PLAYING STYLE: **RIGHT-HAND BAT, WICKET-KEEPER**

NICKNAMES: **THE FINISHER, BOUCH**

SUPERSTAR MOMENT: **BREAKING THE RECORD FOR THE MOST DISMISSALS (CATCHES AND STUMPINGS) IN TEST CRICKET (TWICE!)**

FUN FACT: **AS A KID, BOUCH WAS ALSO A JUNIOR SOUTH AFRICAN SQUASH CHAMPION.**

MARK BOUCHER

Mark Boucher was an old-school wicket-keeper with the safest hands around. Instead of becoming a flashy batter, "Bouch" focused on being South Africa's Mr Reliable behind the stumps.

Across an incredible fifteen-year international career, Bouch took 952 catches and 46 stumpings, as well as playing his part in hundreds of run-outs. If you want to become really great with the gloves then he's definitely the wicket-keeper hero for you.

As a kid growing up in East London, South Africa, Bouch actually started out as a bowler, until one day, aged fifteen, his cricket coach had a brilliant idea: "You've got so much energy and enthusiasm, and you always want to be involved in the game – why don't you become a world-class wicket-keeper instead?"

So, that's what Bouch did! As well as natural catching talent and athleticism he also had the determination to work hard and keep improving his skills. At the start of his Test career in 1998, for example, he struggled against the swinging ball in England, but he soon solved that issue thanks to hours and hours of extra drills after practice. Let that be a lesson to all you young cricketers!

By the early 2000s he had become one of the best in the world and a key part of South Africa's exciting new team, alongside opener Graeme Smith, all-rounder Jacques Kallis and fast bowler Makhaya Ntini. On the cricket field the team was very successful. Bouch was so consistent behind the stumps that he seemed to stop every single ball, no matter how fast, high or wide. He was also capable of spectacular, match-winning moments, like his unbelievable, one-handed diving catch to dismiss Sachin Tendulkar during an ODI match in 2007.

Off the cricket field, however, the team culture was very problematic, with several Black South Africa players suffering discrimination during that time. Years later, in 2021, Bouch apologized for using offensive and racist language towards his teammates, saying, "We are much wiser now and better equipped. We can make amends and we can deal with these important issues better in the future."

Back to Bouch the cricketer – in 2007, he became the first keeper ever to reach 400 dismissals in Test cricket, in only his 104th match. Three months later, his Australian rival Adam Gilchrist overtook him at the top, but Bouch was determined to become the best again. He quickly fought back with more sensational catches and stumpings, and in 2010 he became the first keeper to reach 500 dismissals. It's going to take a very special cricketer to break that remarkable record!

In 2012 Bouch was coming to the end of his career and closing in on an amazing 1,000 international catches and stumpings, when suddenly disaster struck. During a warm-up match ahead of South Africa's series against England a bail flicked up and hit him in the eye. It was a freak accident, and unfortunately the injury was so serious that Bouch was forced to retire early. What a sad end for one of cricket's greatest-ever keepers.

While Bouch will be mostly remembered for his work behind the stumps, we should also mention his very solid batting too. Coming in at number 7 or 8 he played some really important innings when his country needed him most and in 2006 he even scored South Africa's second-fastest century in ODI cricket. With gloves or bat, Bouch was always a great player to have in a high-pressure moment – fierce, focused and totally determined to win.

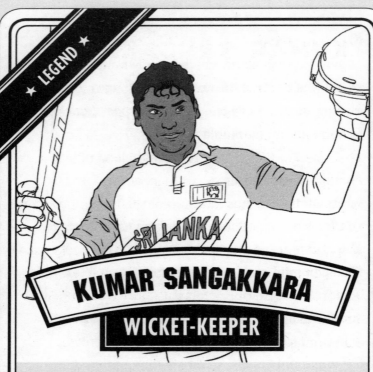

KUMAR SANGAKKARA

WICKET-KEEPER

COUNTRY: **SRI LANKA**

CLUB: **NONDESCRIPTS CRICKET CLUB**

DATE OF BIRTH: **27 OCTOBER 1977**

PLAYING STYLE: **LEFT-HAND BAT, WICKET-KEEPER**

NICKNAME: **SANGA**

SUPERSTAR MOMENT: **WINNING THE 2014 ICC WORLD TWENTY20 FOR SRI LANKA, WITH 52 NOT OUT IN THE FINAL**

FUN FACT: **CRICKET ISN'T THE ONLY SPORT THAT SANGA IS REALLY GOOD AT. WHEN HE WAS YOUNGER HE ALSO PLAYED BADMINTON AND TENNIS FOR HIS COUNTRY.**

KUMAR SANGAKKARA

In 1996, Sri Lanka shocked the cricketing world by beating Australia to win the World Cup. The small island nation of 20 million people was the new champion of the world – unbelievable! At the time "Sanga" was still playing for his country's U-19s team while also studying Law at the University of Colombo. That historic moment, however, inspired him to leave his studies until later and focus on following in the footsteps of the new national heroes: opener Sanath Jayasuriya, middle-order star Aravinda de Silva, and captain Arjuna Ranatunga.

As a batter, Sanga had the talent to combine the best bits of all three – the big hitting of Jayasuriya, the classy strokes of de Silva, and the strong character of Ranatunga. Plus, Sanga wasn't just brilliant with the bat; he was also great with the gloves too. Perfect, two for the price of one – the complete cricketer! Although Sri Lanka's previous wicket-keeper, Romesh Kaluwitharana, was excellent behind the stumps, his batting average was way below 30 runs per innings. It was time for a new kind of keeper-batter to take over.

Sanga made his international debut in 2000, and after scoring 85 runs in only his second ODI against South Africa a new Sri Lankan superstar was born. While he didn't always take as many catches as "Kalu" he made up for that with his magnificent batting, in every form of the game. Oh, and with his sensational stumpings too.

In an ODI against Australia in 2003, Sanga somehow managed to catch a spinning ball from Muttiah Muralitharan and throw the ball at the stumps in one swift movement. Magic!

Test cricket, however, was where Sanga shone most brightly as a batter. As a number 3 he was so good that Sri Lanka often asked someone else to keep wicket so that he could concentrate on doing what he did best: scoring lots and lots of runs. Sanga became the fastest player in the world ever to score 8,000, then 9,000, then 10,000, then 11,000 and finally 12,000 runs. Plus, in 2006, Sanga and his best friend, the middle-order batter Mahela Jayawardene, put on 624 runs against South Africa – breaking the record for the highest-ever partnership in Test cricket.

Sanga loved playing classy strokes all day long, but in March 2009, he had to show his strong character too. As the Sri Lanka players travelled to a match in Pakistan their bus was attacked by gunmen and he suffered wounds to his shoulder. It was a seriously scary experience for him, and the tour was cancelled, but three months later Sanga was back out on the cricket pitch, leading his team to T20 victory against Australia. What a hero!

For over a decade Sanga was consistently one of the best cricketers in the world, but many of his biggest achievements came in 2014. In Tests he hit a career-high 319 against Bangladesh, then 147 against England and 221 against Pakistan. In ODIs he scored another four centuries and eight half-centuries. But best of all, he led Sri Lanka to the ICC World Twenty20 trophy with a man-of-the-match performance against India.

Sanga and his teammates had reached four recent tournament finals, but sadly they had lost every single one. Not this time, though. Playing in his last-ever T20 international, Sanga came in at number 4 and smashed a fantastic 52 off just 35 balls to lead his team to the trophy. When the winning runs were scored he threw his arms up in triumph. Victory, at last! Eighteen years after their success in 1996 it was finally time for Sri Lanka to celebrate again, and the players even carried their hero around the ground on their shoulders. "Sanga! Sanga! Sanga!"

A year later Sanga also ended his ODI career in style, breaking yet another batting record by hitting four centuries in a row at the 2015 World Cup. Sadly, however, Sri Lanka were knocked out in the quarter-finals, and that was it for one of cricket's greatest-ever wicket-keeper batters, who was, in the words of his friend Jayawardene, "The best batter that Sri Lanka has ever produced."

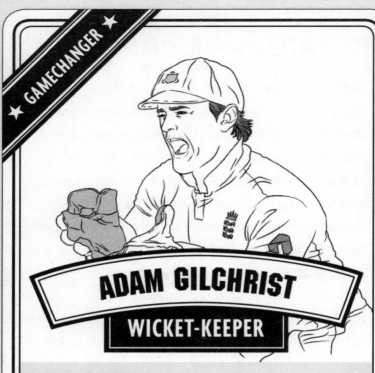

ADAM GILCHRIST

WICKET-KEEPER

COUNTRY: **AUSTRALIA**

CLUBS: **NEW SOUTH WALES, WESTERN AUSTRALIA**

DATE OF BIRTH: **14 NOVEMBER 1971**

PLAYING STYLE: **LEFT-HAND BAT, WICKET-KEEPER**

NICKNAME: **GILLY**

SUPERSTAR MOMENT: **SCORING THE FASTEST-EVER WORLD CUP FINAL CENTURY TO WIN THE TOURNAMENT IN 2007**

FUN FACT: **BETWEEN 1999 AND 2008, GILLY PLAYED IN 96 TEST MATCHES IN A ROW FOR AUSTRALIA WITHOUT MISSING A SINGLE ONE!**

ADAM GILCHRIST

In this book we talk a lot about cricket's gamechangers, but they don't come any greater or more important than Australia's Adam "Gilly" Gilchrist. His impact was so huge that the history of wicket-keeping can be divided into two time periods: before-Gilly and after-Gilly. With his amazing ability to star with both bat and gloves he really did transform the role forever.

And yet Gilly was nearly 25 years old when he played his first international match for Australia, and nearly 28 when he made his Test debut. It wasn't that he lacked the necessary talent; it was just that his country already had a keeper. Ian Healy was one of the best old-school stumpers in the world – a safe pair of gloves and a solid, lower-order batter.

Healy couldn't continue keeping forever, though, and eventually Gilly got his chance to shine, showing off his skills as the first of an exciting new breed of wicket-keeper batters. As well as taking brilliant catches behind the stumps, he was also capable of playing big, big shots, especially in ODIs. Gilly was such a powerful, aggressive hitter that his captain, Steve Waugh, soon moved him up the batting order – from 7, to 6, to 3, and then to 1! That's where he stayed, Australia's star opener, scoring sixteen superb centuries, including one in the biggest game of all.

Gilly had scored important 50s for Australia in the 1999 and 2003 Cricket World Cup finals, but his innings in 2007 was simply spectacular. With the match reduced to only 38 overs each, he came out swinging straight away, smashing the Sri Lanka bowlers for thirteen fours and eight sixes! Not only did he break the record for the fastest century in a World Cup final (72 balls), but he also broke the record for the highest score – 149 (a score which was beaten by Alyssa Healy, Ian Healy's niece, in the 2022 World Cup final!). Gilly followed that up by taking two catches and a stumping, and soon Australia were lifting their third World Cup trophy in a row. What an all-round match-winner!

While Gilly's style was certainly more suited to the one-day game he turned out to be a terrific Test player too. Although he often batted down at number 7 he still managed to score seventeen centuries for Australia (thirteen more than Healy by the way!). Sometimes, he had to rescue his team from trouble after a top-order collapse; and other times his task was to simply speed up the run rate, as he did during the 2006–07 Ashes series against England when he blasted 100 off just 57 balls, one of the fastest Test centuries ever.

But for all his explosive batting brilliance, Gilly will also go down as one of the game's greatest-ever glovesmen. Yes, he was lucky enough to work with excellent bowlers such as Shane Warne and Glenn McGrath who made his life easier, but as a keeper you still have to concentrate and take each and every catch! In 2007 Gilly collected his 396th in only 93 Test matches to overtake Healy as Australia's most successful wicket-keeper. When he retired a year later he finished with a total of 813 dismissals in international cricket, second on the all-time list behind Mark Boucher.

But most importantly, Gilly's gamechanging impact lives on. He showed the world that stumpers can be superstars too, and so a whole generation of young cricketers grew up wanting to become "The Next Adam Gilchrist" – brilliant batters but also incredible keepers.

SARAH TAYLOR

WICKET-KEEPER

COUNTRY: **ENGLAND**

CLUBS: **LANCASHIRE THUNDER, SURREY STARS, SUSSEX WOMEN, WELSH FIRE**

DATE OF BIRTH: **20 MAY 1989**

PLAYING STYLE: **RIGHT-HAND BAT, WICKET-KEEPER**

NICKNAME: **KT**

SUPERSTAR MOMENT: **ANY OF HER LEGSIDE STUMPINGS!**

FUN FACT: **SHE IS IN LOVE WITH HER PUGGLE DOG MILLIE!**

SARAH TAYLOR

Sarah is one of the best wicket-keepers ever, and certainly the greatest female wicket-keeper of all time. Not only that, but she is a graceful batter who would stroke big match-winning runs at big match-winning moments. England were so lucky that she pulled on the Three Lions!

She was so calm with the gloves, standing up to the spinners but also to the pace bowlers – a tricky thing to do! Adam Gilchrist, Australia's superstar wicket-keeper batter, was in awe after watching some of her famous legside stumpings, the batters stranded as she neatly whipped off the bails. She somehow seemed to be able to anticipate the batter's movements before they knew them themselves, and was soon on top with her pin-point reflexes

During her England career Sarah won the 50-over World Cup twice, the T20 World Cup, and the Ashes three times. Not bad! She also eased her way to 6,533 runs, second only to Charlotte Edwards, including six ODI centuries, as well as achieving a world record at the time with 227 dismissals behind the stumps (catches and stumpings). In 2020, she was named by the ICC as a member of the ODI team of the decade, something she is very proud of.

She also broke boundaries, becoming the first woman to play senior club cricket in Birmingham, and the first woman to play an "A" Grade match in Australia for Adelaide's Northern Districts. She was going places!

But unfortunately, things weren't as easy as they looked. Sarah struggled terribly with her mental health and sometimes her anxiety became too much to bear. The problems built up until, during the 2016 T20 World Cup, she ended up spending all her time in her hotel bedroom. She came home and decided to take a break from cricket. It seemed impossible to her that she would be well enough to take part in the 2017 World Cup due to be held in England the following year.

But, bit by bit, the coach Mark Robinson coaxed her back and she was named in England's squad. And what a World Cup she had! She kept wicket brilliantly, including a trademark stumping in the semi-final, and smashed 147 against South Africa in a group game. She then scored vital cameos of 54 in the semi-final, and 45 against India in a thrilling final watched by thousands in a packed Lord's with a television audience of more than 100 million people. Imagine doing *anything* in front of 100 million people!

It was overwhelmingly exciting, and Sarah remembers bursting into tears at Lord's that July evening, realizing how far she'd come. What a journey it had been!

Sadly, her anxiety never truly went away and she retired early from international cricket in 2019 and moved out of the spotlight into coaching, both with Sussex's young wicket-keepers and in a school. Although she was quietly happy she couldn't resist coming back to experience the new Hundred competition, just to see if she still had it. She did! And in the autumn she was named the first-ever women's coach of a men's professional franchise cricket team. Go, Sarah!

MS DHONI
WICKET-KEEPER

COUNTRY: **INDIA**

CLUBS: **COMMANDO CRICKET CLUB, JHARKHAND, CHENNAI SUPER KINGS**

DATE OF BIRTH: **7 JULY 1981**

PLAYING STYLE: **RIGHT-HAND BAT, WICKET-KEEPER**

NICKNAMES: **MAHI, CAPTAIN COOL, THALA (MEANING "LEADER" IN TAMIL)**

SUPERSTAR MOMENT: **LEADING INDIA TO 2011 CRICKET WORLD CUP GLORY**

FUN FACT: **HE'S A MAN OF MANY ELABORATE HAIRSTYLES. HIS HAIR IS A HUGE NEWS STORY IN INDIA!**

MS DHONI

No country in the world is more cricket-crazy than India. Their greatest superstars are treated like national celebrities, with cameras following them everywhere. First there was Sachin Tendulkar, now there's Virat Kohli, and in between there was MS Dhoni.

As a boy growing up in East India, MS actually started out playing football as a goalkeeper for his local team. But one day, his coach had an excellent idea. With such impressive catching and throwing skills perhaps this kid should be playing India's most popular sport instead, CRICKET? It was a totally different game, of course, but MS turned out to be a natural. As the wicket-keeper he just swapped one pair of gloves for a slightly bigger pair, one ball for a much smaller one, and carried on catching.

MS quickly fell in love with wicket-keeping and worked hard on his technique – the diving stop, the turn-and-throw to run a batter out, and his favourite of all, the quick-as-a-flash stumping. It looked like a magic trick, but with plenty of practice, he mastered it. And at the same time, the

more cricket he watched and played, the more MS
wanted to become a big-hitting batter too. Like
all youngsters his ambition was to follow in the
footsteps of his favourite heroes – India's Sachin
Tendulkar but also Australia's Adam Gilchrist.
Yes, MS wanted to become a world-class keeper-
batter too!

He didn't achieve his dream straight away, however. No, at the age of 23 MS was still playing for a local team while also working as a ticket collector on the Indian Railways. But he didn't give up on cricket, and after a few powerful performances for India A with both bat and gloves, suddenly people were talking about him. With his long hair and confident style, was MS about to become India's next big superstar?

It didn't look that way at first. On his ODI debut in 2004 against Bangladesh, MS was run out for a duck after only one ball, and he didn't take any catches as keeper either. Uh oh! But no, the India team believed in him, and in his fifth match against Pakistan MS showed why, smashing 148 runs off only 123 balls. Take that! It was the new highest innings by an Indian wicket-keeper ever, but that record didn't last for long. Just six months later MS went even bigger, blasting an unbelievable 183-not-out against Sri Lanka featuring fifteen fours and ten sixes!

Like his hero Gilchrist, MS was perfect for one-day cricket – brave, powerful and brilliant under pressure. However, he was also able to adapt his style and become a successful Test player too.

And as if batting and keeping wasn't enough work
for one cricketer, MS then became India's captain
in 2007. Did the extra responsibility affect his
performances? No way – if anything it seemed to
make him even stronger!

First, MS led India to victory in the 2007 ICC World Twenty20, and then in 2011, the Cricket World Cup. In the final against Sri Lanka he played perhaps his most important innings of all. With his team chasing 275 to win and Tendulkar and Kohli both already out, he calmly came in at number 5 to score a match-winning 91-not-out. And if there's one moment that sums up MS's style and personality perfectly, it's his final shot. India only needed one run to win, but he didn't even think about a single. Instead, MS went for his trademark helicopter shot (featuring a flick of the wrist that sends the bat in a full circle) and launched the ball for six!

That's MS for you – an entertainer, a winner (he has also lifted the IPL trophy four times as captain of the Chennai Super Kings), and an incredible all-round cricketer. Just in case you still need convincing, here are three records that MS proudly holds and will probably hold for a very long time:

- Most runs in ODI history when batting at number 6 (4,164)
- Most stumpings in international cricket (195)
- Most international matches as captain (332)

ENTERTAINER

JOS BUTTLER

WICKET-KEEPER

COUNTRY: **ENGLAND**

CLUBS: **SOMERSET, LANCASHIRE, MUMBAI INDIANS, RAJASTHAN ROYALS, MELBOURNE RENEGADES, SYDNEY THUNDER, MANCHESTER ORIGINALS**

DATE OF BIRTH: **8 SEPTEMBER 1990**

PLAYING STYLE: **RIGHT-HAND BAT, WICKET-KEEPER**

NICKNAME: **JOSE**

SUPERSTAR MOMENT: **RUNNING OUT MARTIN GUPTILL TO WIN THE 2019 WORLD CUP FINAL!**

FUN FACT: **IF HE WASN'T A CRICKETER, JOS SAYS HE WOULD LIKE TO BE A POSTMAN.**

JOS BUTTLER

At 7.30 p.m. on 14 July 2019, Jos leapt towards the stumps and whipped off the flashing bails. At Lord's cricket ground and all round the world people punched the air, their eyes popping out on stalks! As he threw the ball into the summer sky, followed by his wicket-keeping gloves, and sprinted at full pelt across the grass, he was chased by his ecstatic teammates. Jos had collected the throw that had run out Martin Guptill and won the World Cup for England off the final ball of the super over by "the barest of margins". England were World Champions!

It wasn't Jos's only moment of magic during that World Cup final against New Zealand – the greatest ODI cricket match of all time. He also made 59 in a crucial partnership of 110 with Ben Stokes, scoring at a faster rate than anyone else in the game. When the match ended in a tie, and the rules called for each side to play a super over, Jos and Ben were out again. How did they keep their nerve? Who knows?! You'll have to ask ice man Jos, the man with the coolest head in town.

Jos is one of England's most famous players,

as at home in the coloured clothes of the IPL (he was the MVP of the 2022 IPL) and Big Bash as England's kit. He has unbelievable hand-eye co-ordination and is a batter who can destroy attacks in the time it takes you to run to the cupboard and open a packet of biscuits. He decided to be a wicket-keeper when he was little just so he could be in the game as much as possible! He wasn't a complete natural with the gloves, but worked so hard that England picked him! How about that for ambition?

Jos is very chilled and will play different roles depending on what kind of game he is playing and what the captain wants him to do. In 50-over cricket he's the ideal finisher, terrifying the opposition with his crazy shots – he's one of the best players of the ramp shot in the world and has the fastest ODI century for England (46 balls)! In T20 cricket he opens the innings and tries to get his side off to a rocket-fuelled start – he scored the only century of the 2021 World Cup, against Sri Lanka, reaching it with a casual flick for six off the last ball! In Tests he comes in the late middle order, with instructions to either build an innings or go crazy. He keeps wicket for England in white-

ball cricket and often in Test cricket, though he hasn't had such a great time behind the stumps in red-ball cricket recently.

Jos is a quiet guy, so sometimes he has to make a real effort to be a bossy wicket-keeper telling everyone else what to do. But like his boyhood hero, the Brazilian footballer Pelé, he wanted to grow up to do things no one else could do. We think he's succeeded!

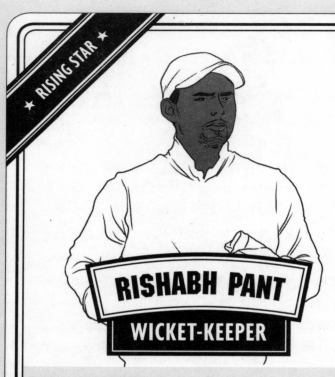

RISHABH PANT
WICKET-KEEPER

COUNTRY: **INDIA**

CLUBS: **DELHI, DELHI DAREDEVILS**

DATE OF BIRTH: **4 OCTOBER 1997**

PLAYING STYLE: **LEFT-HAND BAT, WICKET-KEEPER**

NICKNAME: **SPIDERMAN**

SUPERSTAR MOMENT: **HE SCORED 89 NOT OUT AT BRISBANE IN JANUARY 2021 TO BEAT AUSTRALIA, CLINCHING THE TEST AND THE SERIES**

FUN FACT: **HE RAPS WITH VIRAT KOHLI IN AN ADVERT FOR PIMPLE CREAM!**

RISHABH PANT

Ridiculous! Insane! Audacious! Who would dare reverse-flick Jimmy Anderson for four over the slips? Only one man: Rishabh Pant!

Rishabh just loves hitting a cricket ball. He goes for it, like a puppy launching itself at a bee. His eyes light up and biff! In an India batting line-up full of stars, he is the brightest light.

Rishabh's wicket-keeping may not be as good as his batting yet, but he still holds the joint record for the number of dismissals in a Test: eleven. Not bad for your second skill! He has dropped in and out of the India side because of a few missed catches, but his huge batting talent always brings him back. And his front flips – keep an eye out for them too!

Rishabh first caught people's eye in the IPL. He won a contract with Delhi Capitals when he was just eighteen, the same day that he scored a century for India in the U-19 World Cup. A year later he was picked to play T20s for India and a year after that he played his first Test at Trent Bridge, on India's tour of England. There, he became the first Indian ever to get off the mark in a Test with a six, smashing an Adil Rashid googly back over his head. What a star! Later that series, he made his maiden Test century.

But he properly came of age during India's epic Test series against Australia in 2021, with 97 at Sydney and 89 not out at Brisbane. This helped take India from despair after being bowled out for 36 in the first Test to an incredible series win. Some people had thought Rishabh was just a hard-hitting slogger – he proved he was the real deal!

Rishabh is a true batter of the 2020s. He thrashes the ball all over the ground from the very start of his innings, and it doesn't matter to him whether he is playing in a T20 or a Test match. He doesn't care about his average either, he just wants to have fun and take huge risks – the cheekier the better. Just watch him smile when he is out in the middle – he enjoys every minute!

Sometimes he'll be out cheaply, sometimes he'll drop catches, sometimes he'll take thrillers, but whenever he's in the action, people want to watch. He can change the course of a match in half an hour. We're warning you, don't miss a ball!

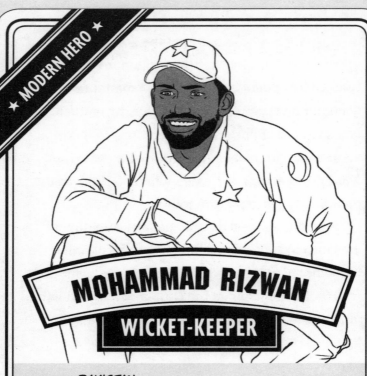

MOHAMMAD RIZWAN

WICKET-KEEPER

COUNTRY: **PAKISTAN**

CLUBS: **KHYBER PAKHTUNKHWA, MULTAN SULTANS**

DATE OF BIRTH: **1 JUNE 1992**

PLAYING STYLE: **RIGHT-HAND BAT, WICKET-KEEPER**

NICKNAME: **RIZU**

SUPERSTAR MOMENT: **SCORING 104 OFF 64 BALLS IN A T20I AGAINST SOUTH AFRICA**

FUN FACT: **HE'S FAMOUS FOR HIS FUNNY COMMENTS. WHEN AZHAR ALI TRIED TO CHASE A CAT OFF THE CRICKET PITCH DURING THE COVID-19 CRISIS, MOHAMMAD TOLD HIM TO STOP, SAYING, "HE HASN'T BEEN TESTED – HE'S NOT IN THE BUBBLE!"**

MOHAMMAD RIZWAN

Unlike most positions on the cricket pitch, you only need one wicket-keeper. So if your team already has a talented player behind the stumps, then sometimes you just have to wait your turn. That was certainly the case with Mohammad Rizwan, Pakistan's next great glovesman.

From 2010 through to 2019, Sarfaraz Ahmed was the country's star keeper, which meant that Mohammad was only seen as a solid back-up. He actually made his international debut in 2015 as a specialist batter instead, but after scoring 67 against Bangladesh his form soon dipped and he was dropped from the team. The role just didn't really suit him; Mohammad had always been a keeper first and a batter second.

The next few years were tough for Mohammad, as he watched Pakistan win the 2017 Champions Trophy without him. He worked hard on his game, though, and kept hoping to make a big comeback for his country. In March 2019, his opportunity arrived and he scored two excellent ODI centuries against Australia, but sadly Mohammad still wasn't selected for Pakistan's Cricket World Cup squad.

It was a crushing blow at the time, but actually it worked out well because after a disappointing World Cup Pakistan decided to make some changes. Suddenly, Sarfaraz was no longer their number one keeper; the gloves were up for grabs!

Mohammad took his chance magnificently and held on tight, as if it was a catch coming towards him at top speed. There's now no doubt that he's Pakistan's number one keeper. Like all greats, he's always busy behind the stumps, talking to his teammates and reacting quickly and athletically to every delivery. Mohammad was excellent in the Test series against England in August 2020, making lots of great stops, stumping Zak Crawley, and taking a wonderful diving catch to dismiss Ben Stokes.

Plus, thanks to lots of practice, Mohammad has become a much better batter too, across all three formats. Coming in at number 7 in Tests, he has played some really important innings for his country, including a determined 95 against Australia, a steady 72 against England and a very impressive 115-not-out against South Africa. If the Pakistan top order fails, Mohammad is there to dig in, stick around and show his strong character.

He can play the big shots too, though. Like his childhood hero, Australia's Adam Gilchrist, Mohammad is now a proper modern keeper-batter, and he even opens for Pakistan in T20I

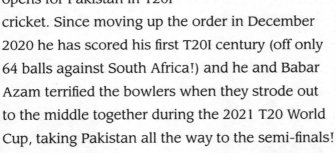

cricket. Since moving up the order in December 2020 he has scored his first T20I century (off only 64 balls against South Africa!) and he and Babar Azam terrified the bowlers when they strode out to the middle together during the 2021 T20 World Cup, taking Pakistan all the way to the semi-finals!

What a cricketing comeback! All that patience has certainly paid off. While Jos Buttler and Rishabh Pant might be more famous at the moment, it's Mohammad who offers the perfect balance between world-class keeping and world-class batting.

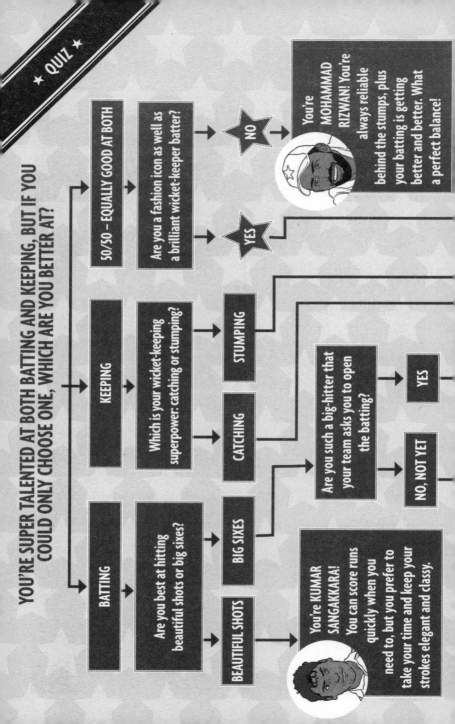

★ QUIZ ★

YOU'RE SUPER TALENTED AT BOTH BATTING AND KEEPING, BUT IF YOU COULD ONLY CHOOSE ONE, WHICH ARE YOU BETTER AT?

BATTING

Are you best at hitting beautiful shots or big sixes?

BEAUTIFUL SHOTS

You're KUMAR SANGAKKARA! You can score runs quickly when you need to, but you prefer to take your time and keep your strokes elegant and classy.

BIG SIXES

Are you such a big-hitter that your team asks you to open the batting?

YES

NO, NOT YET

KEEPING

Which is your wicket-keeping superpower: catching or stumping?

CATCHING

STUMPING

50/50 – EQUALLY GOOD AT BOTH

Are you a fashion icon as well as a brilliant wicket-keeper batter?

NO

YES

You're MOHAMMAD RIZWAN! You're always reliable behind the stumps, plus your batting is getting better and better. What a perfect balance!

Do you bat right-handed or left-handed?

RIGHT

LEFT

You're MS DHONI! You've got style, as well as serious cricket skills. Whether you're catching or batting, you play the game with lots of confidence and superstar quality.

You're SARAH TAYLOR! When that cricket ball flies towards you, you've got the quick reflexes of a cat, plus the skilful glovework to whip off the bails in a flash. BATTER OUT!

You're MARK BOUCHER! With your incredible athleticism and concentration, you can stop every single ball, no matter how fast, high or wide. You've got the safest gloves in the game!

You're RISHABH PANT! Your wicket-keeping still needs a bit of work, but you're young and your batting is so bold and entertaining to watch. The future is yours!

You're ADAM GILCHRIST! You're very good with the gloves and really great with the bat. Put those two talents together and you get an amazing, all-round matchwinner.

You're JOS BUTTLER! You look so calm behind the stumps and when you're walking out to bat, but really, you're a ball-blasting machine. Bowlers, beware – you can play all kinds of crazy, creative shots.

5
SPINNERS

SPINNERS

Right, that's enough about batting and wicket-keeping; it's time to talk bowling! Most cricket teams will have at least five main bowlers, including one all-rounder as we already discussed. Although their aim is always the same – to take lots of wickets – you want to have a range of different bowlers to make life difficult for your opponents. We'll come on to the fast and swinging stuff soon, but first let's look at a slower style that

can bamboozle even the world's best batters. Meet ... the spinners!

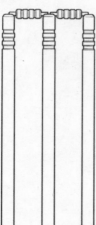

No, they may not look that dangerous with their short run-ups and gentle-looking deliveries, but don't let that fool you. The Top 2 wicket-takers in Test history are both spinners.

THREE THINGS ALL
SPINNERS MUST HAVE:

1 A MAGIC ARM Whether you're bowling **off-spin** or **leg-spin**, you have to be capable of the kind of wicket-taking wizardry that leaves batters wondering, "How on earth did they just do that?"

2 A RANGE OF DIFFERENT, DEVILISH DELIVERIES As a spinner you can't just bowl the same ball every time; if you did, the batter would work you out and blast you all around the ground! So instead you've got to be clever and mix things up – some quicker, some slower, some skiddier, some loopier. Then every now and then you hit them with that extra-special mystery ball of yours, such as the doosra or the googly.

3 PATIENCE Ever heard the phrase "Slow and steady wins the race"? Well, it works perfectly for spinners. Sometimes you might bowl over after over without taking any wickets, as batters blast your slower balls for lots of fours and sixes, but don't despair. To use another famous saying – "Good things come to those who wait."

CRICKET MADE EASY

"OFF-SPIN"

An "OFF-SPINNER" turns the ball from a batter's off stump towards their leg stump if the batter is right-handed, or from their leg stump towards their off stump if they're left-handed.

HOW? Off-spin is bowled with a flick of the fingers.

WHY OFF-SPIN? It's easier to master than leg-spin, and usually a lot more accurate because you have more control over the ball.

WHO HAS BOWLED IT BEST? Muttiah Muralitharan (Sri Lanka), Ravichandran Ashwin (India), Jim Laker (England), Sophie Ecclestone (England; she is a left-arm off-spinner — usually described as slow left arm).

AND WHAT'S THE MAIN MYSTERY BALL? The doosra, a delivery that turns the opposite way to normal off-spin. Though it is a really difficult ball to master legally (without bending your arm), masters of the doosra have included Pakistan's Saqlain Mushtaq and India's Ravindra Jadeja.

"LEG-SPIN"

A "LEG-SPINNER" turns the ball from a batter's leg stump towards their off stump if the batter is right-handed, or off stump to leg stump if they're left-handed.

HOW? Leg-spin is bowled from the back of the hand, with a roll of the wrist.

WHY LEG-SPIN? If you do manage to master it, it's usually more dangerous than off-spin because you have more variety and deception, and can make the ball turn more.

WHO HAS BOWLED IT BEST? Shane Warne (Australia), Anil Kumble (India), Rashid Khan (Afghanistan), Adil Rashid (England), Poonam Yadav (India)

AND WHAT'S THE MAIN MYSTERY BALL? There are quite a few — that's the great thing about wrist-spin — but the trickiest is the googly, a delivery that turns the opposite way to normal leg-spin, but from virtually the same bowling action. Masters of the googly include Pakistani trio Abdul Qadir, Mushtaq Ahmed and Shahid Afridi.

A QUICK HISTORY OF SLOW BOWLING

The first Golden Age of Spin lasted from 1950 to 1970, with legends such as Lance Gibbs and Jim Laker. After that, the fast bowlers took over, but in the early 1990s, spin launched an incredible comeback, led by three exciting new superstars: Anil Kumble, Shane Warne and Muttiah Muralitharan. And it has stayed strong ever since, thanks to new spin kings like India's Ravichandran Ashwin and Afghanistan's Rashid Khan, who has become one of the IPL's biggest superstars.

SPINNER RECORDS

Here are just a few of the amazing bowling records held by spinners:

Spinners with the most wickets in men's Test cricket:

800
Muttiah Muralitharan
Sri Lanka (1992–2010)

708
Shane Warne
Australia (1992–2007)

108
Anisa Mohammed
West Indies (2003 – present)

152
Stefanie Taylor
West Indies (2008 – present)

Most wickets taken by
a spinner in a Test match:

Most wickets taken by
a spinner in a Test innings:

19 OUT OF 20!
Jim Laker
England v. Australia, 1956

ALL 10!
Jim Laker, England v. Australia in 1956
Anil Kumble, India v. Pakistan in 1999
Ajaz Patel, New Zealand v. India in 2021

SO, WHICH KIND OF SPINNER WOULD YOU BE?

Off-spin or leg-spin, googly or doosra? You decide!
But before you go and start mastering your mystery
ball, read on to learn more about eight of the most
successful spinners the world of cricket
has ever seen. Then take
the quiz at the end to
find out which of
these superstars
you would be.

SHANE WARNE

SPINNER

COUNTRY: **AUSTRALIA**

CLUBS: **VICTORIA, HAMPSHIRE, MELBOURNE STARS, RAJASTHAN ROYALS**

DATE OF BIRTH: **13 SEPTEMBER 1969**

PLAYING STYLE: **RIGHT-ARM LEG-SPINNER**

NICKNAME: **WARNEY**

SUPERSTAR MOMENT: **HIS "BALL OF THE CENTURY" AGAINST MIKE GATTING, AT OLD TRAFFORD IN 1993, THE FIRST BALL OF HIS FIRST ASHES TEST!**

FUN FACT: **WHEN HE WAS YOUNGER HIS FAVOURITE SPORT WAS AUSSIE RULES FOOTBALL.**

★ LEGEND ★

SHANE WARNE

He was blond, brash and brilliant! Shane Warne lit up the game like no one else – a rockstar in cricket whites! So when he passed away suddenly in March 2022, aged only 52, the cricket world was in shock. How could they say goodbye to the man who reinvented leg-spin bowling?

Let's go back to the beginning when Shane was invited to the Australian Cricket Academy, where he learned how to bowl the flipper, but was expelled for not keeping to the rules. Ooops! But though Shane didn't like to do what he was told, he was too good to ignore and after only a handful of first-class games for Victoria he was picked to play against India. It wasn't a huge success, he took 1–150, and nor were his next three Tests. But in his fifth, at Melbourne, he bowled the superstar West Indies team out on the last day with 7–52, and Australians started taking notice.

He took seventeen wickets in the next series against New Zealand, and when Australia landed in England for the 1993 Ashes series they were confident they had a new match-winner up their sleeve. Captain Allan Border told Shane not to bowl all his different variations of spin in the warm-up games against the counties, and Australia didn't pick him in the one-day internationals – secret weapons should remain secret, you know! So when Border chucked Shane the ball on the second day of the first Test, none of the English batters knew what to expect. With blobs of sun cream on his nose and upper lip, dyed blond hair and a sparkling earring, Shane didn't look like a serious cricketer. But he was, as England were about to find out!

He tossed his very first ball into the air; it landed in Mike Gatting's blindspot outside leg stump and fizzed back two and a half feet to knock out his off stump. Gatting, a notorious lover of food, looked as if someone had swiped his favourite chocolates and eaten the lot. England captain Graham Gooch later said, "If it had been a cheese roll, it would never have got past him." Mike trudged off and Shane was hugged by his teammates. The world went crazy for that ball and everyone suddenly wanted to bowl leg-spin again.

And from that beginning Shane never looked back. One, two, three, and with a snap of the arm he was off: leg-spinner, top-spinner and repeat.

The only thing more intimidating than his bowling was thinking about his bowling. Shane used to blow batters' minds by pretending that he had invented a new ball before a Test series. What a trickster!

He won the 1999 World Cup with Australia and was part of the world-beating Test side of the early 2000s – one of the greatest of all time. He and fast bowler Glenn McGrath made up one of cricket's best bowling partnerships. Shane was the first man to 700 Test wickets and left international cricket after helping Australia give England one last thrashing: 5–0 in the 2006–07 Ashes.

Gossip and controversy were never far behind Shane: he was fined for telling team secrets to a stranger, and banned from cricket for a year and sent home from the 2003 World Cup after taking a banned drug.

After retiring he became a professional poker player, got engaged to a film star and appeared on *I'm a Celebrity ... Get Me Out of Here!* But cricket remained his greatest passion and he always helped young players out. What a legend.

JIM LAKER

SPINNER

COUNTRY: **ENGLAND**

CLUBS: **SURREY, ESSEX**

DATE OF BIRTH: **9 FEBRUARY 1922**

PLAYING STYLE: **RIGHT-ARM OFF-BREAK BOWLER**

NICKNAME: **JC**

SUPERSTAR MOMENT: **TAKING 19-90 AGAINST AUSTRALIA AT OLD TRAFFORD IN 1956**

FUN FACT: **ON HIS FIRST DATE WITH HIS WIFE, LILLY, THEY WENT TO A CRICKET MATCH!**

JIM LAKER

Only one person in history has ever taken nineteen wickets in a Test match, and it was Jim! Dry-humoured Jim, gruff Jim, who grew up with his aunts in Yorkshire after his dad ran away when he was a baby.

During that famous Test at Old Trafford in July 1956, Jim took 9–37 in the first innings, as Australia were bundled out for 84, and 10–53 in the second. The pitch had been shaved by the groundskeeper under orders from the English chairman of selectors, and the Australians weren't very used to playing off-spin – but even with that help, Jim still bowled like a dream. He sent down over after over of relaxed, gripping, bouncing off-breaks. At the other end, the spinner Tony Lock had to settle for 1–106, much to his irritation!

If you watch some old black-and-white film of Jim bowling in that Test, he just quietly hitches up his trousers each time an Australian is out. When he takes his final wicket, the tenth of the innings and his nineteenth in all, the Australian captain, standing at the non-striker's end, reaches over and shakes his hand. A couple of his teammates can be seen clapping quietly in the background as Jim takes his jumper from the umpire, throws it over his shoulder and ambles off the pitch. Jim! You forgot to celebrate!

On his way home that night he stopped off for a beer and a sandwich at a pub, where lots of

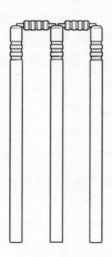

people were standing at the bar and talking about the cricket. Jim quietly sat down and ate his meal and not a single person recognized him. Can you imagine that happening today? His photo would be all over the Internet! That summer he would take 63 wickets against Australia at an average of ten.

Jim's feat will almost certainly never be matched, though leg-spinner Anil Kumble and New Zealand slow left-arm bowler Ajaz Patel have also managed ten wickets in a Test innings. What was Jim's secret? A grip that he changed at will so the batter could never read his hand, a firm tweak of the ball, a variation in loop and a spitting off-break that would turn or skid on.

And it wasn't just in that one game that he shone, Jim's Test record is excellent: 193 wickets in 46 games at an average of just over 21. After he retired he became a commentator, though he never saw another bowler destroy the opposition like he had. And although he died aged 64, he lives on through the most famous bowling figures in cricket.

MUTTIAH MURALITHARAN

SPINNER

COUNTRY: **SRI LANKA**

CLUBS: **LANCASHIRE, CHENNAI SUPER KINGS, RCB**

DATE OF BIRTH: **17 APRIL 1972**

PLAYING STYLE: **RIGHT-ARM OFF-SPINNER/MYSTERY-SPINNER**

NICKNAME: **MURALI**

SUPERSTAR MOMENT: **TAKING 8-70 AGAINST ENGLAND IN 2006**

FUN FACT: **HIS FAMILY RAN A BISCUIT FACTORY.**

MUTTIAH MURALITHARAN

Going into the final day of his final Test match in July 2010, "Murali" had 798 wickets. But it seemed everyone had forgotten the script! Other bowlers kept taking wickets, the Indian tail-enders were holding on, there was a run-out, rain was forecast and the umpire shook his head at an LBW. But just when the spectators had started to give up, India's number 11 edged a catch to slip. Murali was hauled onto his teammates' shoulders and fireworks exploded into the air. Taste that on your tongue – 800 Test wickets!

Yes, mighty Murali took more Test wickets than anyone else – 92 more than even Shane Warne, sitting in second place. He has the most one-day international wickets too: 534. What a bowler! He was a shining gem in the Sri Lankan side during his eighteen-year career, no game was ever dead with Murali in the side, just waiting to get his hands on the ball.

But what was it that made Murali so special? He was an off-spinner, but an off-spinner with a difference. He was born with a disability which meant his right elbow wouldn't straighten no matter what he did. And because of that he ended up not just spinning the ball with his fingers but putting his whole body into the delivery, particularly his powerful, flexible shoulders and his strong wrists. He had very good control of line and length and could bowl marathon spells. A captain's dream!

But people never stopped talking about Murali's elbow. Despite being cleared repeatedly by experts, some still accused Murali of throwing the ball with a bent arm – or "cheating". He was only 23 when an umpire first called "no ball" on Boxing Day at a full Melbourne Cricket Ground. Many people wouldn't have been able to come back from the humiliation – but Murali had undergone tougher tests than that. He was only five when his dad was attacked and the family's biscuit factory burned down during the Sri Lankan civil war.

Murali kept bowling, and learning, and developed a doosra – a ball that spins in the opposite way to a normal off-break. It was banned, and then unbanned, and he took buckets of wickets as batters found it impossible to pick one ball from another. He was a master of disguise!

He has also helped raise money for charity. After a huge tsunami hit Sri Lanka in 2004, Murali organized a convoy of lorries filled with supplies and visited some of the survivors.

Perhaps the highlight of his amazing career was his sixteen wickets against England in the 1998 Test at The Oval – the first Test Sri Lanka won in England. Or the nine wickets in an innings against Zimbabwe – it would have been all ten if one of the fielders hadn't dropped a catch. Whoops! Or Sri Lanka's amazing World Cup win in 1996.

By the time he'd taken his 800th wicket his wrists, shoulders and knees all creaked, but he never lost his huge smile. He's an all-time great whose wicket-taking records will probably never be broken. Take a bow!

RECORD-BREAKER

RASHID KHAN

SPINNER

COUNTRY: **AFGHANISTAN**

CLUBS: **ADELAIDE STRIKERS, SUNRISERS HYDERABAD, TRENT ROCKETS**

DATE OF BIRTH: **20 SEPTEMBER 1998**

PLAYING STYLE: **RIGHT-ARM LEG-BREAK**

NICKNAME: **ROSHI**

SUPERSTAR MOMENT: **BEING NAMED THE ICC MEN'S T20I PLAYER OF THE DECADE IN 2020**

FUN FACT: **HE HAS HIS OWN WICKET CELEBRATION, "THE AEROPLANE", WHICH WAS INSPIRED BY HIS NEPHEWS.**

RASHID KHAN

Warne and Murali are the legends who led the way, but if you're looking for a more modern spin king to copy then let us introduce you to Afghanistan's Rashid Khan. The leg-spinner has been bamboozling batters and breaking records since 2015, when he made his international debut at the age of just seventeen. Rashid has captained his country in all three forms of cricket, but T20 is where he really comes alive. His bowling performances are so magical that in 2020 the ICC even named him the T20I Player of the Decade!

And yet, as a young boy growing up in Nangarhar, Eastern Afghanistan, Rashid's first cricket dream was to be a batter, not a bowler. At the time his country was at war and it wasn't safe to play in the streets, but that didn't stop him from sneaking out to play with his brothers and pretending to be Tendulkar. It was only watching Pakistan's all-rounder Shahid Afridi on TV that changed Rashid's mind about bowling. He loved the way that Afridi played the game – the energy, the excitement and the entertainment. Unlike most spinners he kept things pretty quick: the run-up, the arm action and the speed of the delivery too. Rashid had a new hero, and soon he had a second: India's Anil Kumble, another speedier spinner.

Success didn't come straight away for Rashid. He was actually dropped from the Afghanistan A team and thought about giving up cricket altogether to focus on his studies to become a doctor. Fortunately, though, his mum managed to persuade him to keep playing the sport he loved so much, and before long his performances improved and he was called up to play for his country. In 2016, Rashid represented Afghanistan at the T20 World Cup where he took eleven wickets, the second-most in the whole tournament.

Suddenly, people were talking about his talent. "Rashid Khan is one of the better spinners in this #WT20," influential Indian commentator Aakash Chopra tweeted. "Saying it once again … #IPL teams should pick him immediately." The IPL?! Rashid loved watching the T20 competition on TV, but playing in it – that would be unbelievable, a dream come true. In 2017, Sunrisers Hyderabad won the race to sign Rashid, and who happened to be their bowling coach? Murali! After watching him in the nets the Sri Lankan spin king gave him

the greatest compliment: "Skill-wise, you're better than me." Wow! With Murali's support Rashid picked up an impressive seventeen wickets in his first season, including India's Rohit Sharma,

Australia's Steve Smith, and England captain Eoin Morgan.

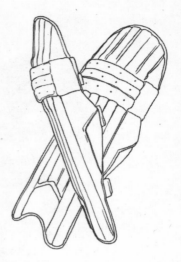

At the age of only eighteen, Rashid was already a cricket superstar, and he was getting better and better. During a T20I against Ireland in February 2017 he bowled two of the best overs you will ever see, picking up five wickets for just three runs! Then three months later in an ODI against the West Indies he took seven wickets for just eighteen runs, one of the Top 5 best bowling figures ever. Rashid's streak continued as he became both the fastest (44 matches) and

the youngest (still only nineteen!) bowler to collect 100 ODI wickets.

So, what are the secrets to Rashid's remarkable spin success? Well, he's so skilful that he can bowl lots of different types of delivery –

the leg-break, the googly, some faster, some slower – and he's so consistent that he can get them right almost every time. Plus, he's so clever at disguising his ball grip that he can keep the batter guessing until it's too late – OUT!

These days Rashid travels the world playing T20 cricket for Afghanistan, as well as for club teams in Australia, England, India, Pakistan, Bangladesh, South Africa and the Caribbean. Not a bad life, eh?

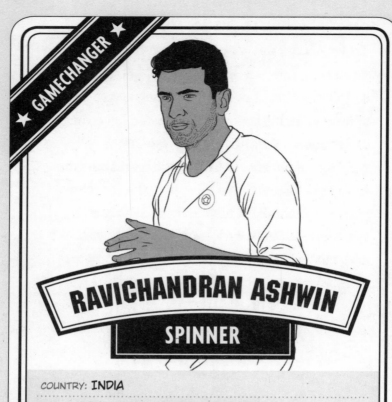

GAMECHANGER

RAVICHANDRAN ASHWIN

SPINNER

COUNTRY: **INDIA**

CLUBS: **TAMIL NADU, DELHI CAPITALS**

DATE OF BIRTH: **17 SEPTEMBER 1986**

PLAYING STYLE: **RIGHT-ARM OFF-BREAK**

NICKNAME: **ASH**

SUPERSTAR MOMENT: **TAKING THIRTEEN WICKETS IN A SINGLE TEST MATCH AGAINST NEW ZEALAND IN 2016**

FUN FACT: **HE HAS A DEGREE IN ENGINEERING.**

RAVICHANDRAN ASHWIN

Spinners are the magicians of cricket, always experimenting and looking for new ways to bamboozle batters. Meet India's latest spin king: Ravichandran Ashwin.

Ravichandran first discovered the "sudokku" ball – an off-spin delivery flicked between thumb and middle finger – while playing in the streets of Chennai. There, they bowled it with a tennis ball, but what if he could do the same with a bigger, harder cricket ball? In 2008, aged 21, Ravichandran saw the Sri Lankan spinner Ajantha Mendis bowl a similar delivery, and that convinced him to give it a try.

And what a successful experiment it turned out to be! Armed with his really accurate off-spinners and his secret weapon sudokku ball, he was now a batter's worst nightmare. Two years later he took the T20 world by storm, starring alongside Murali as the Chennai Super Kings won the IPL and then the Champions League Twenty20 in South Africa.

The timing was perfect. Anil Kumble had recently retired and Harbhajan Singh wouldn't be around forever, so India were looking for a new young superstar spinner. Was Ravichandran ready to step up and shine? Oh yes! He took 2-50 on his ODI debut (against Mendis and Sri Lanka!) and followed that up with 3–24 against New Zealand a few months later. At the 2011 Cricket World Cup, Ravichandran was mostly used as a back-up for Harbhajan, but he bowled well in the two group games he played, helping India to lift the trophy.

Ravichandran was a rising star and soon after that tournament he overtook Harbhajan as India's number one off-spinner. At the 2014 ICC World Twenty20 he was his country's star bowler, taking 4–11 against Australia in the group stage and then 3–22 against South Africa in the semi-final. Unfortunately, he couldn't stop Sri Lanka from winning the final.

It was in Test cricket that Ravichandran really excelled, quickly becoming one of the world's best bowlers. He took nine wickets on his debut against the West Indies in 2011, then twelve against Australia, then thirteen against New Zealand. He grabbed his 100th Test wicket in just his eighteenth match – faster than anyone in the world since 1931, and any Indian bowler in history! Then on the magician marched, past 200, then 300, then 400...

Although Ravichandran's bowling has always been brilliant on the big-spinning wickets of India, he struggled, at first, playing away in countries such as Australia and England. But by practising hard and learning from every experience he has got better and better at adjusting his bowling style to suit different pitches and weather conditions.

Ravichandran doesn't bowl his special sodukku ball as often any more, but when he does he uses it to great effect, as he did against Steve Smith in Australia, and Alastair Cook in England in 2018, bamboozling him in both innings.

Unlike a lot of the other spinners in this section, Ravichandran is also a very handy batter (no offence, Murali!). That's because as a young boy he actually started out as an opener, but after injuring his hip at the age of fourteen he wisely decided that he'd make a better spin bowler instead. Coming in at number 8, Ravichandran hit a century in only his second-ever Test match, outscoring Tendulkar, Rahul Dravid, Kohli and Dhoni! Since then, he's added another four tons, plus one ODI 50. But Ravichandran will always be best known for his incredible inventive bowling.

SOPHIE ECCLESTONE

SPINNER

COUNTRY: **ENGLAND**

CLUBS: **LANCASHIRE, MANCHESTER ORIGINALS**

DATE OF BIRTH: **6 MAY 1999**

PLAYING STYLE: **LEFT-ARM ORTHODOX SPIN**

NICKNAME: **ECCLES**

SUPERSTAR MOMENT: **BECOMING THE NUMBER ONE T20I BOWLER IN THE WORLD IN 2020**

FUN FACT: **SOPHIE LOVES FLYING PLANES AND ONE OF HER NON-CRICKET DREAMS IS TO BECOME A PILOT ONE DAY.**

SOPHIE ECCLESTONE

Can you call someone a "rising star" when they're already the number one ODI and T20I bowler in the world? Maybe not, but Sophie Ecclestone has even bigger ambitions for the future: to become not just one of the greatest spinners, but one of the greatest women's cricketers to ever play the game.

Sophie started playing cricket at the age of just seven. She was the only girl in the local junior club at the time, but that didn't stop her. Nothing could stop her. She was such a talented spinner that at school she even surprised her headmaster by bowling him out first ball! By the age of sixteen, Sophie was called up to play for her county, Lancashire, and she also travelled to Sri Lanka to train with her England heroes.

Sophie learned lots from that amazing experience, and a few months later she was making her England debut and taking her first international wicket. Wow, it was all happening so fast, and Sophie was still at school! She had to miss the 2017 Cricket World Cup to finish her exams and without her, England went on to win the whole tournament. Nooooo!

Never mind, Sophie would just have to win another one when she got the chance! In the meantime she worked harder than ever to become England's best spinner. In 2018, she took 4–37 in an ODI against India, and then 4–18 in a T20I against New Zealand.

That soon became Sophie's favourite format. In T20 cricket, bowling isn't just about taking wickets; it's also about stopping your opponents from scoring lots of quick runs. And with her accurate left-arm spin, there's no one better at frustrating batters. It's almost impossible to hit Sophie for six, and when you try you usually get out!

At the 2018 ICC Women's World Twenty20, Sophie was very solid but not yet spectacular. She did bowl Australia's Alyssa Healy with a beautiful delivery in the final, but sadly it wasn't enough and England were easily defeated.

They didn't win the 2020 ICC Women's T20 World Cup either, but this time Sophie really took the tournament by storm. She claimed 3–7 in one match against the West Indies, and on top of her eight wickets – the third-highest total – her fifteen overs went for only 49 runs. That's just over three runs per over, which is remarkable in T20 cricket!

And Sophie's World Cup achievements didn't end there. By the end of the tournament she had become the youngest woman to reach 50 T20I wickets, and, best of all, the number one T20I bowler in the world!

But Sophie still wasn't done. Although she had a terrible start to the 2022 World Cup in New Zealand, Sophie bounced back to finish as the leading wicket-taker in the whole competition. She bowled England to victory in the semi-final, with 6–36 against South Africa, and although England were beaten by Australia in the final, Sophie had proved herself a superstar in the making.

ADIL RASHID

SPINNER

COUNTRY: **ENGLAND**

CLUBS: **YORKSHIRE, BANGLA TIGERS, ADELAIDE STRIKERS, NORTHERN SUPERCHARGERS, PUNJAB KINGS**

DATE OF BIRTH: **17 FEBRURARY 1988**

PLAYING STYLE: **LEG-BREAK BOWLER**

NICKNAME: **RASH**

SUPERSTAR MOMENT: **WINNING THE WORLD CUP WITH ENGLAND IN 2019, AND GETTING RUN OUT FOR ZERO IN THE FINAL SO THAT BEN STOKES COULD GET THE STRIKE BACK!**

FUN FACT: **HIS BEST FRIEND IS ENGLAND'S MOEEN ALI.**

ADIL RASHID

Get your binoculars: Adil is a rare breed – an English leg-spinner. Even more unusually, Adil is internationally successful. In fact, he has taken more Test wickets than any other English leg-spinner for 70 years. Amazing!

It hasn't always been easy though. In his first bowl in Test cricket, against Pakistan in October 2015, he had a nightmare, taking no wickets and conceding 163 runs. However in the second innings he whistled out five players for 64 and nearly bowled England to an amazing win. Ups and downs! His Test career has wobbled about since, due to some inconsistent performances, not being picked and a series of injuries, particularly to his shoulder – a vital part of a leg-spinner's action.

In white-ball cricket, though, Adil is one of the best in the business. He has been a crucial part of England captain Eoin Morgan's plans as he rebuilt England's limited-overs sides. Eoin told him, "What we expect from you is that you create chances." Adil was happy with that, sending down overs packed with a fast-turning pick 'n' mix of leg-breaks, googlies, top-spinners and sliders.

Adil doesn't mind whether he bowls at the start of the innings with the new ball or later on – he just loves bowling. He can send the ball down quite fast when he wants to, once topping 70mph, and says it is the pivot in his bowling action which gives him "the snap". He is an attacking bowler who doesn't get too discouraged if he is pinged down the ground – and he seems to have amazing powers over India's superstar Virat Kohli, who keeps getting out to him.

Adil started bowling leg-spin when he was only eight, with the encouragement of his dad, who converted the cellar of their Bradford house into a rudimentary winter net. His dad pushed him to be the best he could be and reminded him how tough it would be for a young Asian boy to make it through the system. But Adil burst into the Yorkshire side when he was only eighteen, at the seaside town of Scarborough, taking six wickets against Warwickshire on his debut. He's stayed with Yorkshire ever since, though he only plays white-ball cricket for them these days.

He's taken over 150 one-day international wickets, including eleven during England's heart-thumping 2019 World Cup campaign. Adil's most memorable contribution in the final was sprinting a second run to get Ben Stokes down the right end to face the last ball of the match (before the super over). Adil was run out for zero, without facing a ball, but it was all worth it in the end! After England had won the trophy Adil went back to Bradford, where he was given a hero's welcome!

YOU'RE A TOP WICKET-TAKER, BUT HOW DO YOU PREFER TO BOWL?

FINGER-SPIN

WRIST-SPIN

YOUR OWN SPECIAL KIND OF SPIN

Spin bowling is your special talent, but can you bat too?

Do you prefer to spin the ball fast or vary your pace?

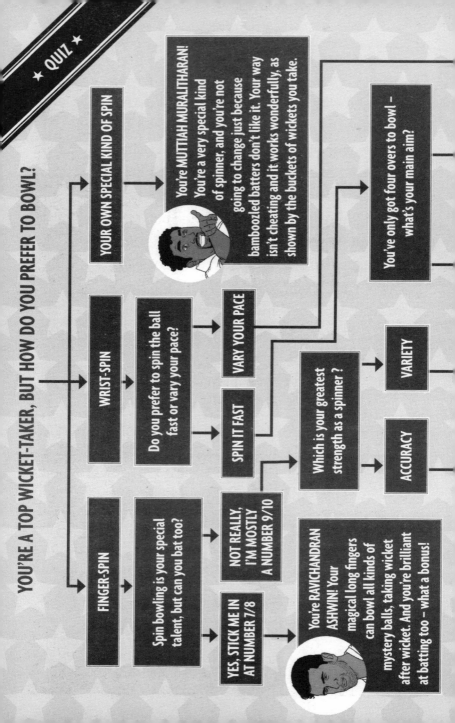

You're **MUTTIAH MURALITHARAN!** You're a very special kind of spinner, and you're not going to change just because bamboozled batters don't like it. Your way isn't cheating and it works wonderfully, as shown by the buckets of wickets you take.

YES, STICK ME IN AT NUMBER 7/8

NOT REALLY, I'M MOSTLY A NUMBER 9/10

SPIN IT FAST

VARY YOUR PACE

You've only got four overs to bowl – what's your main aim?

You're **RAVICHANDRAN ASHWIN!** Your magical long fingers can bowl all kinds of mystery balls, taking wicket after wicket. And you're brilliant at batting too – what a bonus!

Which is your greatest strength as a spinner?

ACCURACY

VARIETY

TAKING LOTS OF WICKETS

STOPPING THE BATTERS FROM SCORING

You're **SHANE WARNE!** You're such a spin king that speed doesn't really matter. A short run-up and a flick of the wrist is all it takes for you to move the ball around as if by magic.

You're **ADIL RASHID!** You're an attacking bowler, so you don't worry if a batter smashes you for six a few times. You've got so many different quick-spinning deliveries that you'll get them out in the end.

You're **SOPHIE ECCLESTONE!** You might not turn the ball as much as other bowlers, but batters find it seriously hard to score runs against your amazingly accurate spin. And when they try to go big, you usually get them out.

You're **JIM LAKER!** You're a classic old-school spinner who's in the team to do what you do best – bowl! Tweaking the ball with your skilful fingers, you love tricking the batter with a range of different deadly deliveries.

You're **RASHID KHAN!** You're such a clever and consistent spinner that it's almost impossible to smash your balls for six. And once batters get frustrated, the wickets usually soon follow.

6
FAST
BOWLERS

FAST BOWLERS

And last but not least, it's time for … the fast bowlers! Although they're often the last names on the batting line-up, they're the first to grab the new ball and take wickets.

THREE THINGS ALL FAST BOWLERS MUST HAVE:

1 LONG ARMS AND LONG LEGS Fast bowlers tend to be very tall because that way the ball leaves their hand at a greater height and so bounces up at the batter. The award for tallest bowler of all time goes to Mohammad Irfan from Pakistan, who is a massive 7ft 1in, or 2.16m tall! Or if this is easier to picture, the height of 86 Creme Eggs stacked on top of each other.

2 SUPER SPEED Well, duh! Fast bowlers build up pace in two ways: through their run-up and through the power in their body. Another Pakistani bowler, Shoaib Akhtar, holds the official record for

the longest run-up – 23 steps. But the real world-record holder, according to Guinness, is his fellow countryman Sameer Khan Yousufee, who in 2020 travelled over 4km (or 2.5 miles) before bowling the ball.

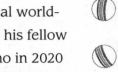

3 A SCARY SCOWL For when a batter hits them for six!

THREE KEY DELIVERIES FOR EVERY FAST BOWLER:

1 BOUNCER A delivery bowled shorter so that it bounces up towards the batter at about head height.

2 SLOWER BALL A delivery that is a lot slower than your usual speed in order to surprise the batter.

3 YORKER A difficult delivery that should land right at the batter's feet. Get it a little wrong, and you'll probably get slogged for six; but get it right, and it's absolutely unplayable!

THE SPEED SCALE

Fast bowling isn't all about pace and power. Not all the time, anyway. In fact, many batters really like facing the fastest bowlers because they know that if they manage to hit the ball it will fly away for four runs. So, sometimes it's a good idea to slow things down and aim for accuracy and control. That's why in cricket we find a wide range of speeds and styles, all the way from medium through to fast:

MEDIUM (70—75MPH) Nathan Astle, Marcus Stoinis

MEDIUM-FAST (75—80MPH) Sam Curran, Colin de Grandhomme

FAST-MEDIUM (80—85MPH) Stuart Broad, James Anderson, Glenn McGrath, Jason Holder

FAST (85+) Dennis Lillee, Michael Holding, Shoaib Akhtar, Allan Donald, Brett Lee, Jofra Archer, Kagiso Rabada

As well as using different speeds, fast bowlers also make the ball move in different directions, using **seam**, **swing** and **reverse-swing**.

CRICKET MADE EASY

"SEAM", "SWING" AND "REVERSE-SWING"

"SEAM" BOWLING is where you make sure that the ball lands on the seam (the dotted stitching around the middle).

WHY? It can cause the ball to move in or away from the batter when it bounces.

HOW? Hold the seam upright in your hand as you bowl.

"SWING" BOWLING is where you get the ball to move in the air, changing direction as it heads towards the wicket.

WHY? The idea is to trick the batter, and so the later the ball swings the better!

HOW? Hold the seam at a slight angle. You'll need a new ball that's shiny on one or both sides.

"REVERSE-SWING" BOWLING is where the ball moves in the opposite direction to normal, e.g., inswinging instead of outswinging.

WHY? Same as swing bowling — to make it harder for the batter!

HOW? You'll need an older ball, where one side is shiny and the other is scuffed up. Keep polishing the shiny side!

FAST BOWLER RECORDS

Here are some of the fastest bowlers in cricket:

Top 3 fastest deliveries ever bowled:

100.2MPH
Shoaib Akhtar
Pakistan v. England (2003)

100.1MPH
Shaun Tait
Australia v. England (2010)

99.9MPH
Brett Lee
Australia v. New Zealand (2005)

Top 3 male fast bowlers with the most wickets in Test cricket:

640
James Anderson
England (2003 – present)

563
Glenn McGrath
Australia (1993–2007)

537
Stuart Broad
England (2007 – present)

Top 3 female fast bowlers with the most wickets in ODI cricket:

252
Jhulan Goswami
India (2002 – present))

180
Cathryn Fitzpatrick
Australia (1993–2007))

178
Shabnim Ismail
South Africa (2007 – present)

Best figures for a male fast bowler in an innings:

9 WICKETS FOR ONLY 28 RUNS
George Lohmann
England v. South Africa, 1896

Best figures for a female fast bowler in an innings:

7 WICKETS FOR ONLY 22 RUNS
Ellyse Perry
Australia v. England, 2019

SO, WHAT KIND OF FAST BOWLER WOULD YOU BE?

Seam or swing, fast or fast-medium? Would you go for extra speed or extra control? To help you make up your mind, here are the stories of eight superstar fast bowlers who've taken lots of wickets in different ways. Then take the quiz at the end to find out which of these superstars you would be.

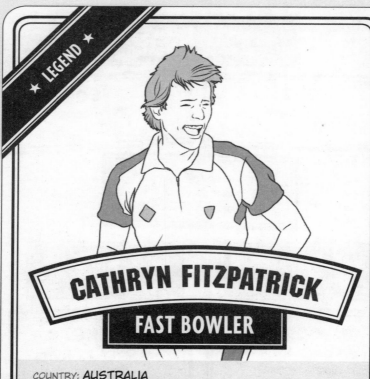

CATHRYN FITZPATRICK

FAST BOWLER

COUNTRY: **AUSTRALIA**

CLUB: **VICTORIA**

DATE OF BIRTH: **4 MARCH 1968**

PLAYING STYLE: **RIGHT-ARM FAST**

NICKNAME: **FITZ**

SUPERSTAR MOMENT: **PLAYING IN AND WINNING THE 1997 AND 2005 WORLD CUP FINALS**

FUN FACT: **SHE USED TO BE A REFUSE COLLECTOR AND A POSTWOMAN!**

CATHRYN FITZPATRICK

Meet a living legend. Cathryn, all 5ft 6in of her, was the fastest female bowler of her, or any other, time. Regularly sending down 77mph bullets, her blonde hair flying in her wake, she spearheaded Australia to two World Cup victories. She was also a vital cog in one of the greatest female teams of all time. What a badass!

In her early years Cathryn was fast but wild, a tangle of arms and legs and a wonky radar. But she met women's coach John Harmer who remodelled her action – imagine taking your bike apart and putting it back together so it worked better! Now she was unstoppable, out-swinger after out-swinger pitching in the right place, scaring the living daylights out of the poor batters. And she was very, very, difficult to score off.

Cathryn had a crucial role in helping Australia to two World Cup wins, in 1997 and in 2005. In 1997, she took three for eighteen to knock out India from their own competition in the semi-final on Christmas Eve in Delhi. She also generally tormented England's batters. She finished with 60 wickets in thirteen Tests for Australia and 180 one-day international wickets – a record at the time.

She kept fit by taking a succession of physical jobs, from running behind the bin lorry to delivering the post. This built up her strength as well as giving her more time for training in the afternoons – unfortunately for her opponents. And not until the very end did she earn any money for playing cricket. In fact, she and her teammates used to have to leave their jobs to go on tour and pay for the tour themselves. Thank goodness things have changed for female cricketers!

When at last she retired after sixteen years at the top, she moved into coaching. Was the quiet assassin any good? You guessed it! She took the top job with Australia's women's team and led them to victory in the 2012 and 2014 T20 World Cups and the 2013 World Cup. Go, Cathryn!

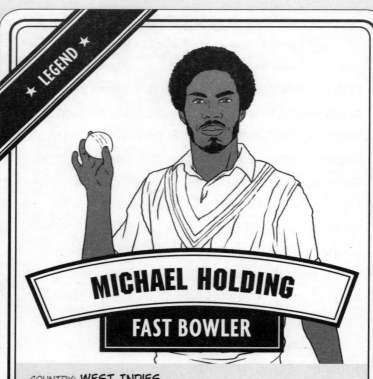

MICHAEL HOLDING

FAST BOWLER

COUNTRY: **WEST INDIES**

CLUBS: **JAMAICA, DERBYSHIRE**

DATE OF BIRTH: **16 FEBRUARY 1954**

PLAYING STYLE: **RIGHT-ARM FAST**

NICKNAME: **WHISPERING DEATH (COOL, RIGHT?)**

SUPERSTAR MOMENT: **TAKING FOURTEEN WICKETS IN A TEST MATCH AGAINST ENGLAND IN 1976**

FUN FACT: **AFTER RETIRING FROM CRICKET HE RAN A PETROL STATION IN HIS HOMETOWN OF KINGSTON CALLED "MICHAEL HOLDING'S SERVICE CENTRE".**

MICHAEL HOLDING

In the days before speed guns, big screens and batting helmets were everywhere, fast bowlers were just fast. Scarily fast. The golden age of pace bowling began in the 1970s, with Australia's Jeff Thomson and Dennis Lillee, and Andy Roberts and Michael Holding of the West Indies. All four were speedy, successful bowlers, but we're going to focus on the one they called "Whispering Death". Don't worry, we'll explain the awesome nickname a bit later on, but first let's tell you about Holding himself.

Michael was born in Kingston, Jamaica, into a cricket-mad family. His dad signed him up as a member of the local Melbourne Cricket Club when he was still just a toddler! That turned out to be a wise decision, though, as Michael grew up to become a fast bowler with great potential. Speed, strength, height and accuracy – he had everything necessary to become a wicket-taking superstar.

Michael made his international debut in 1975, just months after the West Indies had won the first-ever Cricket World Cup. There was a lot of pressure on him as the new kid in the team, but he kept himself calm and his deliveries dangerous. Although

Australia won the Test series Michael won the pace race, bowling balls at up to 97mph, even faster than Thomson, Lillee and Roberts. Wow!

Michael was off to an impressive start, and things got even better when the West Indies toured England in 1976. Before the first Test, the England captain Tony Greig made the big mistake of insulting his opponents. "I am not really sure they're as good as everyone thinks they are," he said, before claiming that his team was going to make the West Indies players "grovel", a word with strong racist associations. Greig's comments made the West Indies players really angry, and even more determined than ever to win.

Michael knew exactly how he was going to fight back: with the ball. As he glided in to bowl with his smooth, long, almost silent strides, the England batters weren't expecting him to release it at such scorching, ferocious speed. See, that's why they called him "Whispering Death"! Some of his deliveries were bouncers aimed at the body, but most were missiles aimed at the stumps. It was terrifying stuff and it soon led to lots of wickets: seven in the second Test, and then fourteen in the fourth! Yes, at The Oval in London, Michael ripped through the

England batting line-up twice, finishing with 14–149, still the best match figures ever by a West Indian in a Test match. "Whispering Death" was now the most dangerous fast bowler in the world.

Over the next eleven years Michael went on to terrify lots more batters with his fierce, fast bowling, in Tests and also ODIs. He ended his international career in 1987, with a total of 391 wickets, as well as a 1979 Cricket World Cup winner's medal.

What next for "Whispering Death"? Michael decided to try being a TV cricket commentator instead. He turned out to be a total natural, talking intelligently about cricket, as well as lots of other important issues. In July 2020, for example, Michael made a very passionate speech about his experiences of racism: "I'm 66 years old. I have seen it; I have been through it and I have experienced it with other people. It cannot continue like this."

To achieve equality, Michael called for "good people to stop being silent" and instead speak out against racism. His strong message was heard all over the world, in sport and beyond, making a powerful impact, just like his fierce, fast bowling did back in the day.

★ LEGEND ★

JAMES ANDERSON

FAST BOWLER

COUNTRY: **ENGLAND**

CLUB: **LANCASHIRE**

DATE OF BIRTH: **30 JULY 1982**

PLAYING STYLE: **RIGHT-ARM FAST-MEDIUM**

NICKNAME: **JIMMY**

SUPERSTAR MOMENT: **TAKING 11-71 AGAINST PAKISTAN IN 2010**

FUN FACT: **HIS HOME CLUB, OLD TRAFFORD, RENAMED ONE END OF THE GROUND "THE JAMES ANDERSON END" IN HIS HONOUR.**

JAMES ANDERSON

"Jimmy" has taken more Test wickets than any other England player. In fact, he has taken more Test wickets than any other fast bowler from any country. What a champion! Not bad for a shy boy from Burnley who used to do the scoring for his dad's local team.

Even as he enters his fourth decade, Jimmy still wants to play more Tests for England. He seems to have drunk a magic potion: the older he gets, the better he bowls. Amazing!

But the secret is that Jimmy wasn't actually very good until he had a growth spurt in his teens and started bowling a lot quicker. He signed for Lancashire where he learned how to swing the ball, but it took him six months to be brave enough to speak in the dressing room.

He was picked for England after his first full season with Lancashire and was selected for the World Cup in South Africa, where his booming out-swingers took four match-winning wickets against Pakistan and made people's ears prick up.

But Jimmy wasn't there yet. His England career was up and down over the next few years.

His peculiar bowling action – he looked at the ground when delivering the ball – perplexed the England coaches and they tried to change it. Bad move. Jimmy ended up with a stress fracture in his back and when he came back to Lancashire they told him to go back to his old ways. He did.

And so Jimmy started the second half of his career: an intelligent bowler who doesn't give away many runs, who can swing the ball both ways and nip it off the seam. In he runs: bang, the ball lands on the same spot delivery after delivery. No wonder the batters get frustrated! He developed a ball with a wobble seam that keeps the batters guessing, and has become excellent at reverse-swing. He passed 500 Test wickets, then 600, while leading the England attack with his old buddy Stuart Broad. Not that he celebrated much; Jimmy is famously grumpy!

He won a Wisden Cricketer of the Year award to celebrate a breakthrough year in 2008 when he took boxes of wickets, including 9–98 against New Zealand at Trent Bridge. At the same ground in 2010, he took eleven wickets against Pakistan, who were hypnotized by his bowling. That winter he was a vital part in England winning the Ashes, snatching 24 Australian wickets. And so it continued, until the winter of 2022, when Jimmy was dropped for England's tour of the West Indies. He wasn't happy, but continued to practise hard at home, and was picked for the first Test of the summer by new England captain Ben Stokes.

He is a specialist number 11 with the bat but has had his moments in the sun, including a record tenth wicket stand against India with Joe Root, and batting for over an hour to save the Cardiff Test against Australia in 2009.

He had success in white-ball cricket, but Test cricket is where he rules supreme. He's the king of the swingers!

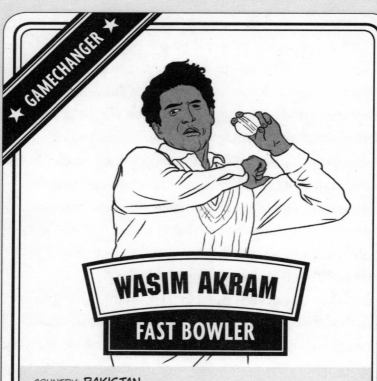

WASIM AKRAM

FAST BOWLER

COUNTRY: **PAKISTAN**

CLUBS: **PAKISTAN INTERNATIONAL AIRLINES, LANCASHIRE**

DATE OF BIRTH: **3 JUNE 1966**

PLAYING STYLE: **LEFT-ARM FAST**

NICKNAME: **KING OF SWING**

SUPERSTAR MOMENT: **WINNING THE 1992 WORLD CUP WITH PAKISTAN AND BEING NAMED MAN OF THE MATCH IN THE FINAL**

FUN FACT: **EX-ENGLAND BOWLER MIKE SELVEY CALLED HIS DOG WASIM IN HIS HONOUR.**

WASIM AKRAM

Want to meet the greatest left-arm bowler ever?
Step this way! Wasim terrorized batters throughout
the 1990s with his swing and seam bowling at
a blistering pace. And together with his Pakistan
teammate Waqar "Toe-Crusher" Younis made one
of the best opening bowling partnerships in history.

Wasim was not only fast (over 90mph) and
ferocious, he also had a thrilling bouncer (though
not for the batters!) and a clever slower ball.
Worse, he would hide the ball as he ran up so the
batters couldn't guess which way he was going
to swing it. What a nightmare! He took 414 Test
wickets at an average of 23.62 along with 502 ODI
wickets, but even more important than that was
his aura – Wasim could take a wicket with just
a swish of his lush black mop of hair.

Wasim could use an old battered ball just as
cunningly as a shiny new one. The brilliant Imran
Khan had taught him the secrets of reverse-swing.
In fact, Wasim and Waqar were so good at reverse-
swing on the tour of England in 1992, and England
were so bad at playing it, that Pakistan were
accused of cheating. Hmmm. A few years later,

everyone wanted to know how to bowl reverse-swing, including the English!

Young Wasim grew up in Lahore, where he loved playing cricket, especially the fast and furious evening street games. He was plucked from those to a summer camp for Lahore's best young players, and from there to attend a Pakistan U-19 camp. There he bowled at Pakistan captain Javed Miandad, who was so impressed that just two months later eighteen-year-old Wasim was playing for Pakistan!

In his second Test, at Dunedin in New Zealand, he took 10–128. He was on his way! He spent

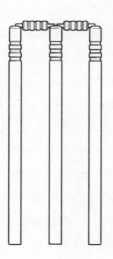

a year in Durham playing league cricket, and learning how to bowl in English conditions – English batters soon wished he hadn't! He took buckets of wickets, in both Tests and ODIs, and could biff the ball with the bat, scoring three Test centuries, including a whopping 257-not-out against Zimbabwe.

Perhaps the highlight of Wasim's career was winning the World Cup with Pakistan in 1992. In the final against England he took 3–29, including two wickets in two balls, which knocked a huge hole in the English batting line-up. His teammate Aaqib Javed later said, "Those two deliveries were unplayable. It was perfect reverse-swing." Wasim was named man of the match.

Wasim was made captain of Pakistan but match-fixing rumours spoiled the second half of his career. He retired at 36 after Pakistan flopped at the 2003 World Cup, the owner of the most wickets of any left-arm pace bowler, and possibly the best ODI bowler ever. As he put away his whites for the last time, the batters of the world let out a huge sigh of relief. What a bowler!

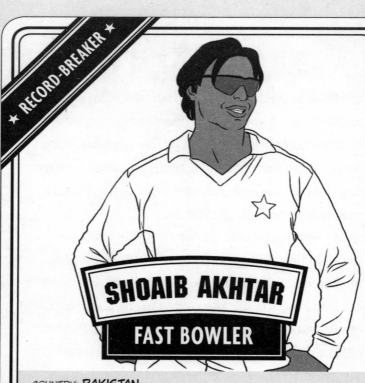

SHOAIB AKHTAR

FAST BOWLER

COUNTRY: **PAKISTAN**

CLUBS: **ISLAMABAD LEOPARDS, KOLKATA KNIGHT RIDERS, DURHAM**

DATE OF BIRTH: **13 AUGUST 1975**

PLAYING STYLE: **RIGHT-ARM (VERY) FAST**

NICKNAME: **THE RAWALPINDI EXPRESS**

SUPERSTAR MOMENT: **BOWLING THE FASTEST BALL IN THE HISTORY OF INTERNATIONAL CRICKET AT THE 2003 CRICKET WORLD CUP**

FUN FACT: **SHOAIB WAS ONCE SUSPENDED FROM SCHOOL FOR RIDING HIS MOTORBIKE THROUGH THE HEAD TEACHER'S OFFICE!**

SHOAIB AKHTAR

If you're a fan of super speed, then Shoaib Akhtar is the cricket superstar for you. Whether riding his motorbike or racing in to bowl, his aim has always been simple – to go as fast as he possibly can. Oh, and take a lot of wickets along the way!

As a young boy growing up in a very poor part of Rawalpindi in northern Pakistan, Shoaib built up his strength by throwing bricks on the mountains near his home. As he started to bowl, he switched the bricks for smaller rocks instead. That meant that when he finally began to practise with a proper cricket ball it must have felt as light as a feather!

With his amazing arm strength, supreme self-belief and a long, scary run-up, Shoaib was a superstar in the making. He made his debut for Pakistan in 1997, but it was only two years later in India that Shoaib really made a name for himself. The story goes that before the Test match started he saw Sachin Tendulkar, India's star player, practising in the nets and asked him, "Do you know who I am?" When Sachin shook his head, Shoaib replied, "You soon will."

It was a very confident thing for a young cricketer to say, but that was Shoaib's style, and he backed it up with some incredible bowling. First, he charged in and knocked Rahul Dravid's leg stump right out of the ground with a brilliant yorker. That brought Tendulkar in to bat, and with his next ball Shoaib did it again, although this time it was the middle stump that went flying. He had done it; not only had he taken the wicket of the world's greatest batter, but he had got him out for a golden duck!

When Shoaib bowled like that, with such pace and aggression, he was terrifying and totally unplayable. He was regularly reaching speeds of 95mph, but he decided that wasn't enough. Shoaib wanted to go even faster; he wanted to bowl cricket's first-ever 100mph ball. He believed that he had done it against New Zealand in 2002, but sadly it wasn't accepted because the official speed gun wasn't working. "I can deliver over 100mph any day," Shoaib declared afterwards, as confidently as ever. He would just have to show his speed again.

Now, all good stories need a rival, and for Shoaib that was Australia's Brett Lee. He too was getting closer and closer to that 100mph mark as both bowlers arrived at the 2003 World Cup. So, who would be crowned the fastest bowler in the world? In the end, Lee took more wickets and lifted the World Cup trophy, but it was Shoaib who won the pace race. In his second over against England his deliveries just got faster and faster: 98.4, 98.5, then 99.1mph...

Shoaib was so close to achieving his aim; it was time for one last push: "I said, okay this is the time, just cross the barrier, finish it for the rest of my life." For his last delivery of the over Shoaib gave it everything he'd got: 100% energy in the run-up, and then 100% aggression and arm strength as he reached the wicket and bowled. The batter, Nick Knight, was able to flick it away, with no idea that he had just faced the fastest ball in cricket history.

"Look!" Shoaib said, pointing up at the speed on the scoreboard – 100.2! It was official; he had just become the fastest bowler of all time.

JOFRA ARCHER
FAST BOWLER

COUNTRY: **ENGLAND**

CLUBS: **SUSSEX, RAJASTHAN ROYALS, HOBART HURRICANES**

DATE OF BIRTH: **1 APRIL 1995**

PLAYING STYLE: **RIGHT-ARM FAST**

NICKNAME: **JOFRADAMUS**

SUPERSTAR MOMENT: **BOWLING THE SUPER OVER TO HELP ENGLAND WIN THE 2019 WORLD CUP**

FUN FACT: **JOFRA IS SUCH CLOSE FRIENDS WITH SUSSEX AND ENGLAND TEAMMATE CHRIS JORDAN THAT THEY EVEN OWN A DOG TOGETHER – A FRENCH BULLDOG CALLED GRIFFIN!**

JOFRA ARCHER

Jofra was born on the Caribbean island of Barbados. Despite loving football and the long jump as well, he decided to focus on cricket. But just as he was all set to follow in the large footsteps of legendary West Indies bowling speedsters such as Michael Holding and Curtly Ambrose, disaster struck. After making his debut for the national U-19 team, Jofra picked up a bad back injury that kept him off the cricket pitch for two long years. At one point, doctors even told him that he might never play again.

However, Jofra didn't give up on his cricket dream, and once the pain reduced he came racing back. Although he couldn't quite reach the same speeds as he had before, he was still scary enough to impress Chris Jordan during a nets session in Barbados. Like Jofra, Chris had been born on the island but he had moved to London as a young boy, and so he played international cricket for England instead. "You should do the same," Chris suggested to Jofra.

Soon, Jofra was setting off on his journey to England in the hope of becoming a cricket superstar. He started out playing in the local leagues, but before long he had worked his way up to join his best friend Chris in the Sussex First XI.

Despite his back injury Jofra's high arm action still enabled him to put lots of pace and bounce on the ball, reaching up to 95mph. His bowling wasn't just about scary speed, though; he also had amazing accuracy and variety. He could bowl brilliant bouncers and yorkers all game long, as well as a special slower knuckle ball that really bamboozled batters.

With all that exciting talent, Jofra was all set to become a world T20 superstar. As well as Sussex, he also starred for Hobart Hurricanes in Australia's "Big Bash" and the Rajasthan Royals in the IPL. In India, he got to play alongside England's star all-rounder Ben Stokes, who said, "Jofra Archer is the most naturally gifted bowler I've ever seen."

The timing was perfect because the 2019 Cricket World Cup was coming up, and after three years of living in England Jofra was now available to play for the national team at last. Even though he was still new to ODIs he was just too lethal to leave out! And with the pressure on, he proved it:

3–27 against South Africa

3–29 against Bangladesh

3–30 against the West Indies

3–52 against Afghanistan

3–52 against Sri Lanka

By the end of the group stage, Jofra had already become England's new leading wicket-taker in a World Cup! He grabbed two more in their semi-final win against Australia, including their captain Aaron Finch for a golden duck. England were through to the final!

Although Jofra only managed to add one more wicket, he still played a crucial role in the game. After 50 overs each, both teams had scored 241 runs,

and so for the first time ever the World Cup final would be decided with a super over! First, Ben Stokes and Jos Buttler went in to bat for England, and they scored fifteen off their six balls.

Could New Zealand beat that? With the pressure on, the England captain, Eoin Morgan, handed the ball to his coolest bowler – Jofra! His super over started badly, with a wide, then two runs, and then a six! Uh oh, suddenly New Zealand only needed seven runs off four balls to win. But Jofra didn't panic; he kept calm and carried on bowling, until it all came down to the last ball. Martin Guptill just had to score two runs to win it for New Zealand, but no, Jofra managed to limit him to one – England were the Cricket Champions of the World! Jofra collapsed to the ground, punching the air with passion. He had done it; the determined boy from Barbados had bowled his way to the top, and now he had won the Cricket World Cup!

KYLE JAMIESON

FAST BOWLER

COUNTRY: **NEW ZEALAND**

CLUBS: **AUCKLAND, CANTERBURY KINGS, ROYAL CHALLENGERS BANGALORE**

DATE OF BIRTH: **30 DECEMBER 1994**

PLAYING STYLE: **RIGHT-ARM BAT, RIGHT-ARM FAST-MEDIUM**

NICKNAME: **KILLA**

SUPERSTAR MOMENT: **TAKING 6-7 FOR CANTERBURY KINGS, THE THIRD-BEST BOWLING FIGURES IN T20 HISTORY**

FUN FACT: **HE'S A BIG NBA FAN AND PLAYED BASKETBALL AS A KID BEFORE CHOOSING CRICKET.**

KYLE JAMIESON

Fast bowlers are usually the tallest players on the cricket pitch, but even so, Kyle Jamieson still towers above the rest. At 6ft 8in he's second only to Pakistan's man-mountain Mohammad Irfan, who takes the world title at somewhere between 6ft 10in and 7ft 1in, depending on which info you choose to believe. But that's enough about Jamieson's height; let's talk about his talent.

As a kid in Auckland, Kyle actually started out as a batting all-rounder, but as he grew and grew it became clear that he was born to be a fast bowler instead. The switch took time and lots of coaching sessions, but in 2019 at the age of 24 Kyle was finally ready to really let the ball fly and bounce. His big breakthrough moment came for the Canterbury Kings in New Zealand's Super Smash when he took six wickets in his four overs, for only seven runs, the third-best bowling figures in T20 history!

Kyle finished the tournament as the leading wicket-taker, and a year later he was called up to play for New Zealand. Some people thought that he was only in the national team to bring height and bounce to the attack, alongside Trent Boult,

Matt Henry and Tim Southee. But in fact, Kyle delivered a whole lot more, outbowling all three. On his ODI debut in January 2020, he took two key wickets and won the Player of the Match award. And when he made his Test debut two weeks later he took four wickets in the first innings, including India's captain Virat Kohli.

But Kyle was only just getting started:

5–45 v. India

7–77 v. the West Indies

11–117 v. Pakistan, the third-best match figures in Kiwi cricket history!

After six Tests Kyle already had 36 wickets, and the whole cricketing world was talking about New Zealand's exciting new speedster. He's keeping his feet on the ground, though. "I'm still a long way off where I want to be as a bowler and as a cricketer," he said in a post-match interview. "I think in the next year or so, I'm going to make massive strides." Batters, beware!

Whether he meant the "massive strides" part as a joke about his height or not, he's definitely a man on a wicket-taking, match-winning mission. In June 2021, Kyle took 5–31 in the first innings of the World Test Championship final to help New Zealand become officially the best team in the world.

While Kyle is currently bowling at around the 85mph mark, he believes that he can add some extra speed to go with the bounce and swing. Plus, he also has ambitions to become an all-rounder again. In the past a lot of fast bowlers have been famously bad batters, but not Kyle. He already has a Test match 50 to his name, and he's aiming for many more. And why not? Kyle is quickly becoming a new cricket superstar.

★ RISING STAR ★

ISSY WONG

FAST BOWLER

COUNTRY: **ENGLAND**

CLUBS: **WARWICKSHIRE, CENTRAL SPARKS, BIRMINGHAM PHOENIX, SYDNEY THUNDER**

DATE OF BIRTH: **15 MAY 2002**

PLAYING STYLE: **RIGHT-ARM (VERY) FAST**

NICKNAME: **WONGI**

SUPERSTAR MOMENT: **WINNING THE 2019 WOMEN'S TWENTY20 CUP WITH WARWICKSHIRE**

FUN FACT: **SHE'S SMART AS WELL AS SPEEDY. SHE CAN SOLVE A RUBIK'S CUBE IN UNDER 17 SECONDS!**

ISSY WONG

As you've recently read, Shoaib Akhtar became the first male bowler to reach 100mph back in 2003, but the pace race is still on in the women's game. So far, no female bowler has broken the 80mph barrier, but nineteen-year-old Issy Wong is speeding her way towards that target, one ball at a time.

Issy started playing cricket at primary school, and by the age of eleven, she was already representing her county, Warwickshire. Bowling was always her special talent, and the faster the better. She loved nothing more than outpacing the other boys and girls around her. Oh, and taking lots of wickets too, of course!

In 2017, Issy was there in the crowd at Lord's watching as the England Women's team beat Australia to win the World Cup. What an inspiring moment for a young cricketer to witness! Two years later, Issy helped Warwickshire to win the U-17s national title and the Women's Twenty20 Cup (taking three wickets in one win against Cricket Wales), as well as becoming the youngest-ever player in the Women's Cricket Super League.

Issy's not just a rising star; she's a rising superstar!
In 2020, aged eighteen, she was even called up to
train with the England squad, alongside lots of her
World Cup heroes.

It's been a whirlwind journey so far, but Issy
isn't afraid of anything. When she first met Tim
MacDonald, the national bowling coach, he

asked her about her goals for the future. "I want to be the first Englishwoman to bowl 80mph," she replied straight away. Why not? She's already bowling at well over 70mph, and with more coaching and practice she's only going to get quicker and quicker.

To go with her exciting speed, Issy also has tons of style too. In her short career so far she has already shown off a range of different haircuts and colours, usually worn with one of her trademark bandanas. Although she hasn't made her senior England debut yet, Issy spent the winter of 2021–22 playing for Sydney Thunder in the Women's Big Bash – what an opportunity for a teenager! Issy's on a fast track to the top, no doubt about it.

★ MODERN HERO ★

MARIZANNE KAPP

FAST BOWLER

COUNTRY: **SOUTH AFRICA**

CLUBS: **EASTERN PROVINCE, SYDNEY SIXERS, PERTH SCORCHERS, OVAL INVINCIBLES**

DATE OF BIRTH: **4 JANUARY 1990**

PLAYING STYLE: **ALL-ROUNDER, RIGHT-HAND BAT, RIGHT-ARM MEDIUM**

NICKNAME: **KAPPIE**

SUPERSTAR MOMENT: **SHE WAS PLAYER OF THE MATCH IN THE FIRST-EVER HUNDRED FINAL**

FUN FACT: **SHE IS MARRIED TO HER TEAMMATE AND SOUTH AFRICA'S CAPTAIN DANE VAN NIEKERK.**

MARIZANNE KAPP

As well as being an amazing cricketer, Marizanne is a fitness freak. Seriously! And it's not surprising when you look at her childhood. Her parents both ran marathons, and to relax after a long day they would take their children for 1km sprints! Then there was swimming before school and after school. And football and rugby with her cousins outside in the road. And then a session in the gym every evening after high school.

As well as being extremely fit, Marizanne is a naturally talented athlete who represented her province in cricket, netball, cross-country, swimming, biathlon and lifesaving. Phew! Time for normal people to have a lie-down on the sofa. But not Marizanne. And of all the sports she threw herself into, cricket was the one she liked best.

She loves to keep busy, so it is no surprise that she is an all-rounder and always involved in the game: a fast-medium swing bowler and an attacking batter who has a ODI century and scored the most runs for South Africa in the 2018 World Cup in the West Indies.

Marizanne was only nineteen when she was first picked, at a time when women's cricket in South Africa didn't offer much of a career path. Her mum looked at the prospects for female cricketers and advised her to get a real job!

Later, when Cricket South Africa eventually offered their female players contracts, Marizanne was one of the first six players on their list! She is quiet and shy and a devout Christian, and doesn't enjoy the limelight, but through her example has helped transform the sport for girls in South Africa.

Marizanne was only the third woman to take an international T20 hat-trick, against Bangladesh, and she also took a hat-trick for Sydney Sixers in the Women's Big Bash. Everyone laughed because she kept such a straight face while her teammates were celebrating around her.

In 2018, Marizanne married Dane van Niekerk, her South African captain and teammate. The two of them had known each other for years – they were the first girls to join a boys' cricket academy in South Africa, and then made their debuts for South Africa just a few days apart. They have also played together for Sydney Sixers in the Women's Big Bash League – though Marizanne has admitted that it is sometimes tricky when one of them does well and the other doesn't! When they both batted together in the T20 World Cup in 2018, they became the first married couple to bat in international cricket. How cool is that!

Early on, their families struggled to accept their relationship, but now everyone gets on well and loves their pet dog, Loki! You might have seen Marizanne bowl the first-ever ball in the Hundred in the summer of 2021. She also took the first wicket before finishing the competition as player of the match in the final, helping the Oval Invincibles to the title with 26 and then 4–9 in eighteen unplayable balls of out-swing. All this in front of 17,000 people at Lord's. Just another awesome milestone!

YOU'RE A FANTASTIC FAST BOWLER, BUT WHAT'S YOUR MOST DANGEROUS WEAPON?

SUPER SPEED

Do you go around telling everyone you want to become the fastest bowler of all time?

YES

NO, BUT THAT WOULD BE NICE

Your need for speed goes beyond the cricket pitch too, but what would you rather be fast at: riding a motorbike or solving a Rubik's cube?

SOLVING A RUBIK'S CUBE

RIDING A MOTORBIKE

When you retire, would you rather become a cricket coach or a commentator on TV?

COACH

COMMENTATOR

SWING

Are you better at bowling in longer or shorter forms of cricket?

LONGER

SHORTER

In terms of speed, would you describe your bowling as medium-fast or fast?

MEDIUM FAST

FAST

EXTRA BOUNCE

Do you get your extra bounce from being really tall or having a high-arm action?

BEING REALLY TALL

A HIGH-ARM ACTION

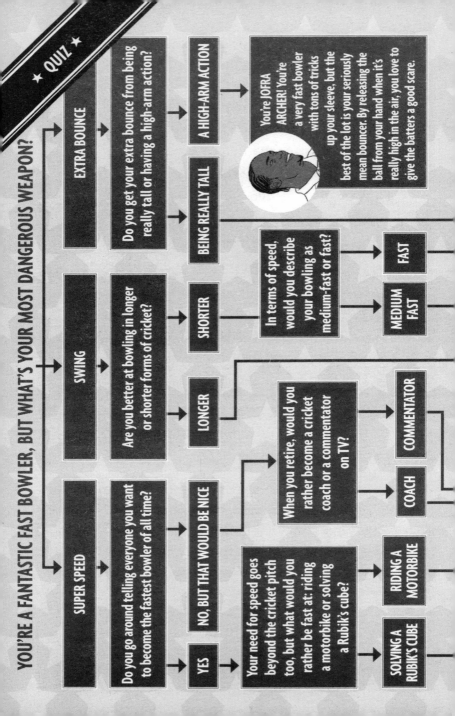

You're JOFRA ARCHER! You're a very fast bowler with tons of tricks up your sleeve, but the best of the lot is your seriously mean bouncer. By releasing the ball from your hand when it's really high in the air, you love to give the batters a good scare.

You're ISSY WONG! You're smart as well as speedy, and you've got tons of style too. You're on a fast track to the top, no doubt about it.

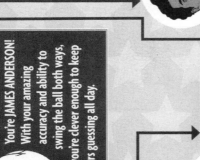

You're JAMES ANDERSON! With your amazing accuracy and ability to swing the ball both ways, you're clever enough to keep the batters guessing all day.

You're KYLE JAMIESON! While your height does give you some extra bounce as a bowler, that's far from your only strength. You can also swing the ball beautifully and your yorker is brilliant too.

You're MICHAEL HOLDING! Your voice is as super-smooth as your speedy bowling, and hopefully, you can use it to speak up about important issues such as discrimination, as well as cricket.

You're WASIM AKRAM! As a bowler, you've got it all: variety, pace, bounce, and best of all, swing. Which type of delivery will you go for next? No one knows! Batters breathe a big sigh of relief when it's someone else's turn to bowl.

You're SHOAIB AKHTAR! You're already super-quick, but your aim is to go even faster. With your amazing arm strength, supreme self-belief and a long, scary run-up, you're a bowling superstar in the making.

You're CATHRYN FITZPATRICK! You want to share your experience and your seriously fast bowling skills with the next generation, and help them to win too. Good luck!

You're MARIZANNE KAPP! You might not be the fastest bowler in your team, but who needs speed when you can swing the ball with such wizardry? Oh, and you're a talented batter, too!

OVER AND OUT

So, there you have it – the stories of 50 of the game's most entertaining and successful players. Ultimate Cricket Superstars, over and ... OUT!

We hope you've enjoyed reading all about these amazing heroes, their inspiring life stories and their greatest moments in the game. See, cricket really is incredible, isn't it? The sixes and centuries, the hat-tricks and "HOWZAT!"'s, and above all, the exciting drama that comes when two teams desperately try to bowl each other out. What's not to love about that?! Plus, hopefully we've shown you that cricket really isn't that complicated, especially now that you know your hook shots from your helicopter shots, and your spin from your swing.

But before we say goodbye and good luck, it's time for you to answer the ultimate question – after learning about lots of different styles, positions and personalities, which kind of cricketer do you want to be? The next:

DAVID WARNER, bravely batting first against the fastest bowlers?

 **JOE ROOT**, making lots of runs beautifully in the middle order?

ELLYSE PERRY, starring with both bat and ball?

 **SARAH TAYLOR**, taking every catch behind the stumps?

RASHID KHAN, bamboozling batters with your range of spin?

 **JOFRA ARCHER**, terrifying batters by bowling bouncers at top speed?

MARIZANNE KAPP, swinging the ball all over the place?

Whatever you decide, we really hope that this book will inspire you to pick up a bat and ball and have a great time playing the game with your friends. So, who wants to bat first?

GLOSSARY

Baggy green The Australian cricket cap.

Ball tampering Trying to illegally alter the ball to make it easier for the bowlers to take wickets (see Sandpapergate!).

Boundary The rope or board around the ground that marks the edge of the playing area. To add to the confusion, a ball that crosses this rope is also known as a boundary — that's a four or a six.

Century A hundred runs. A huge milestone in cricket.

Crease A line across the pitch, four feet from the stumps — where the batter stands.

Doosra A Hindi word that means "other". It is the finger-spinner's googly, meaning it turns away from the right-handed batter. Notoriously difficult to bowl without bending the arm illegally.

Flipper A leg-spinner's ball that looks as if it is going to pitch short but skids on low and fast and gets the batter in all kinds of trouble.

Four A shot that touches the ground at least once before crossing the boundary. Adds four to the batter's score and handy if you're in a run-chase.

Googly The wrist-spinner's classic trick – it turns towards the right-handed batter, when they are expecting the opposite. An essential tool for a good wrist-spinner.

Hat-trick Three wickets in three consecutive balls by the same bowler. Usually in the same over but can span two overs or, sometimes, two innings! Time to bring out your best bowling celebration!

Howzat! The bowler's appeal to an umpire, meaning – is that out? Can be a question, or a demand!

Innings A side's turn to bat.

IPL (Indian Premier League) The most famous and richest T20 cricket league in the world. Played, surprise, surprise, in India!

Match-fixing Illegally trying to fix a match a certain way for money. Cricketers who are caught usually get a ban.

No-ball If a bowler steps the whole of their foot over the front crease, the umpire calls "no-ball" and the bowler has to bowl again. If you are out off a no-ball it doesn't count – cue a very angry bowler!

Off-break/off-spin The most common ball bowled by a finger-spinner. When bowled by a right-handed bowler, it moves towards a right-handed batter's legs.

Out! The cry a batter doesn't want to hear! Means walking back to the pavilion, your innings finished.

Over Six balls in a row bowled by the same bowler.

ICC (International Cricket Council) In charge of the game.

One-day international (ODI) A limited overs match of 50 overs for each team that takes place on one day.

Partnership The runs scored between two batters.

Power play A period during a limited-overs game when the fielding side has to have a certain number of fielders in the 30-yard (inner) circle. This should make it easier for the batting side to score runs.

Sandpapergate An example of ball tampering, involving the Australian cricket team during the Cape Town Test of March 2018. Cameron Bancroft was spotted by the TV cameras trying to alter the state of the ball with a piece of sandpaper that he was storing down his trousers. Painful!

Six A shot that crosses the boundary without hitting the ground and the quickest way to wake up a sleepy crowd. Signalled by the umpire raising both arms into the air – we hope they've remembered to put on their deodorant!

Slog A wild swing at the ball in an attempt to hit a boundary. Often played by tailenders who think they won't last long at the crease so they might as well have a go.

Strike rate For batters – the number of runs they score per hundred balls. For bowlers – the number of deliveries the bowler needs to take a wicket.

Stumps The three sticks a batter stands in front of and protects. Bails (smaller sticks) sit on top of the stumps.

Test match An international match that can last up to five days. Considered the most difficult of all forms of cricket.

The Ashes A series of Tests played between England and Australia. Named the Ashes because when England first lost at home to Australia, a newspaper ran a joke obituary of English cricket. The next time England toured, a bail was burnt and put in a trophy and given to the England captain. Usually played every two years, alternating between countries.

The Hundred A 100-ball cricket tournament that was launched in England and Wales in 2021. Eight city-based sides play a women's and men's competition. Unusually for cricket there are no overs, just ten balls bowled from each end before switching.

T20 cricket Twenty-over-a-side cricket. It was first played professionally in the UK in 2003 and is now the most popular form of cricket in the world.

Wicket One of those confusing cricket words which can mean the pitch, the stumps or a dismissal. If your side loses a wicket, it means one of your batters is out.

ACKNOWLEDGEMENTS

First of all, a huge thanks to our editors Daisy Jellicoe and Charlie Wilson and our agent Nick Walters for guiding us all the way from an idea to an actual book.

Thanks, Tanya, for being such a joy to work with. Polite cricket claps also go to: Calmore Cricket Club, the Cavaliers, the Winchester nets gang, Tom for all those back garden games, Mum for all those hours of driving and supporting, and Dad for passing on his love of the sport and all West Indies teams. Arlo, get ready – you're up next.

M.O.

Kudos to Matt, for being such a brilliant person to write a book with; to Tim de Lisle, Raf Nicholson and Stanley Wilkinson for lending me their brains; and to Andy, Rosy, Sonny, and especially Dylan, for putting up with selection discussions over the breakfast table.

T.A.

ABOUT THE AUTHORS

MATT OLDFIELD dreamed of becoming the next Dimitri Mascarenhas. Sadly, his bowling was never that brilliant and neither was his batting, so he decided to try telling stories about sport instead. He writes the bestselling Ultimate Football Heroes series with his brother Tom. He is also the author of the Johnny Ball: Football Genius series. In 2020, he won the *Telegraph* Children's Sports Book of the Year for *Unbelievable Football*. Now, at last, after years of badgering his editors, he has written a book about his other favourite sport, cricket.

TANYA ALDRED grew up playing cricket in the garden with her three brothers and huge extended cricket-obsessed family. Their dogs, guinea pigs and rabbit dodged balls and gave friendly licks when the batters were out. Being truly hopeless didn't stop her loving the game and she ended up writing about it, mostly for the *Guardian*. She has co-written one other book for children, *The Legend of Sparkhill*, with England all-rounder Moeen Ali.